ON FIFTH AVENUE

LORD ROSEBERY'S
NORTH AMERICAN JOURNAL
1873

LORD ROSEBERY

Lord Rosebery's North American Journal—1873

Edited by A. R. C. Grant
with Caroline Combe

Foreword by Roger Fulford

ARCHON BOOKS

Copyright © 1967 by A. R. C. Grant

First published in U.S.A. by
ARCHON BOOKS
The Shoe String Press, Inc.
Hamden, Connecticut

Library of Congress Catalog Card No: 68-13132

Printed in Great Britain

Contents

List of Illustrations

7

Plates IV to VI and VIII to XI and the Endpapers are reproduced by courtesy of the Curator of the Picture Collection, The New York Public Library, Circulation Department, and Plate VII by courtesy of the J. Clarence Davies Collection, Museum of the City of New York.

Foreword by Roger Fulford

A TEN-WEEK tour of America and Canada, which was made almost a century ago by a shrewd, amusing and engaging young Englishman, is the theme of this attractive book. It has been prepared by the writer's great grandson, Mr Antony Grant, and the reader can sense at once that he is moving across the Atlantic with a companion who is not only highly entertaining but completely original. Disraeli, who met the traveller a year or two afterwards when he had returned from a later visit to America, said that he was "as full as an egg of fun and quaint observation".

In his introduction Mr Grant has outlined for us the eventual career of the writer of the journal. In the future Lord Rosebery was to be prime minister, and to win lasting renown with a number of books on historical personalities; these were largely of the eighteenth century, but they included a most understanding and penetrating portrait of Lord Randolph Churchill. All that lay in the future, for the diary transports us to a time before Rosebery was famous, when he was still in his middle twenties. (In 1873, when the tour was made, he was twenty-six.) On the very first page we are conscious of the fun of youth. He travelled from Euston on the Irish Mail and the rough ride over the western slopes of England burst a bottle of champagne concealed in his bag—and it burst all over the weighty tomes of de Tocqueville's history of the United States.

Throughout the diary his descriptions of scenery are splendid, whether he is describing a storm at sea—"the huge waves chafing

about as if irresolute what to destroy"—or the Chaudière falls,
which he watched as the sun set and "stilled the waters to glass".
The deftness with which he depicts personality is remarkable in
so young a man. Though always appreciative of those he meets—
whether it is a guard on the railway or a Canadian politician—he
allows his diary to reveal the sharper tang to his character. Here,
for example, are his comments on an illustrious member of the
Astor family—presumably W. B. who was known as "the land-
lord of New York". "Coming out of church I was shewn Mr
Astor, a hard, dreary looking old man and the richest in the
world". The pathos of wealth seems summed up in the word
"dreary looking". Living at Dalmeny, which is just outside Edinburgh, the young man shows that he had not failed to observe his
fellow Scots with a somewhat severe eye. Of a Canadian statesman
of Scottish origin he writes, "he is an obstinate-looking, long
upper-lipped Scotchman, with the peculiarly aggravating unintelligent manner of an intelligent, middle-aged Scot". Of a
Scottish minister speaking at the St Andrew's dinner at New
York he writes, "when I heard the well-known accents, and saw the
wonted shake of the polemical pow I knew my fate".

His narrative seems to escape those trivialities and wounding
comparisons between American and European civilization which
mar so many works of this nature. In one passage he describes the
appalling behaviour of an Englishman in a hotel and he admits that
he has dwelt on it "perhaps unduly" because he wants to give himself a lesson against hasty judgement which would have led many
people to conclude that the unmannerly ogre was an American and
to draw deductions from this false premise which would have been
wholly unfair. He surprises us by drawing attention to the respect
for authority which he notices among the Americans. He illustrates
this by an anecdote about a juror who, without grumbling or
whining, was kept waiting for a quarter of an hour while the chief
justice of New York (Daly) discoursed to Rosebery about
meteorology (of all completely irrelevant topics). Perhaps this
kindly and understanding view of the Americans is partly explained
by the friendships he made in that country—notably with Sam

Ward. The life and times of Ward, who lived from 1814 to 1884,
have been recently and entertainingly recorded.[1] By birth and
training a banker, Ward ran through fortune after fortune. His
first wife was an Astor, his sister was Julia Ward Howe—author of
the Battle Hymn of the Republic—his greatest friend was Longfellow and his nephew—the novelist Francis Marion Crawford—
drew his portrait in his novel *Dr Claudius* as Mr Bellingham.
Himself a mathematician, poet, diplomat, lobbyist, classicist, linguist, "forty-niner" Ward was at the centre of all that was best and
worst in his age. Rosebery's other close friend in the United States
was William Hurlbert—the extremely civilized editor of the New
York *World*. Together the three friends formed the "Mendacious
Club" of which Ward was president, Hurlbert the "Liar" and
Rosebery the "Sycophant".

We learn from the journal that Rosebery was a tolerably intrepid
traveller; he thought nothing of rising at what he calls "the genial
hour of 4.30" and at another early morning start he complains that
he found his hotel "nothing but draughts and housemaids".

Again this journal is enjoyable because Rosebery is always himself, always perfectly natural; he never seems to strike an attitude
or to write for effect. He visits Chicago two years after the disastrous fire (traditionally supposed to have been started when Biddy
Maloney's cow kicked over a lantern in a wooden shed) in which
17,000 buildings were destroyed. He describes the marvellous
resurrection of the city and regrets that he could not stay longer to
see more of it, but he makes it quite clear that his real regret was
that he could not stay for one more day to see the celebrated
Goldsmith Maid running in a trotting race. (This was an under-
standable and honest regret for one who later in life was to lead in
the winner of the Derby.) And naturally the journal is throughout
enriched by many delightful shafts of his wit—that irrepressible
sense of humour about which Queen Victoria was to warn him
twenty years later—"Lord Rosebery is so clever that he may be
carried away by a sense of humour, which is a little dangerous".
We may or may not agree with the Queen, but in this case

1. Lately Thomas; *Sam Ward, king of the lobby*; Houghton Mifflin, 1965.

the danger did not go beyond the writer and the paper of his journal.

Readers of the book can hardly fail to be surprised by the number of members of the English aristocracy travelling about America whom Rosebery chanced to meet. These encounters are not unlike the meeting of friends in a saunter up St James's Street. "Just outside Chicago I met a train in which I saw the Duke of Manchester's head." A few days later "here I saw a figure that I felt sure I knew. It was Bertie Mitford (afterwards Lord Redesdale). We parted at luncheon at the St James's Club 9 or 10 months ago". And again, "we dined at Evanston in Utah where I met Skelmersdale on his way home". On leaving the Niagara Falls he meets "the Alfred Churchills" (Sir Winston's great-uncle and aunt). Then he was introduced to "an elderly Weld of Lulworth who is drawn here by his love of canvas-back shooting". He attends a dance in New York for "the Princess Royal"—that was the facetious name for the daughter of President Grant—and says that there were a whole lot of old Etonians there "and I am afraid we cronied together too much". The time was just starting when the young Englishman went to America in search of a bride, and male members of the aristocracy at this time were not unlike Disraeli's heroes Alfred Mountchesney and Lord Milford who—it may be remembered— on their way to Scotland for the shooting "reconnoitered the heiresses in their course". There is no evidence that Rosebery had any such motive in his travels. He seems to have come through them unscathed and even emerges heart-whole from the frightening experience of travelling home with "two Miss Potters", one of whom was later the formidable Mrs Sidney Webb.

What then drew him to America? No doubt in part there were the same reasons which drew all the friends he mentions meeting— travel without the menace of language, beautiful country and spectacular achievements, but in his case there was something more. Rosebery was in some ways curiously shy. With his circle of English friends, and even with his family, he was extremely reserved and indeed always gave the impression—as his son-in-law says—that he loved seclusion for its own sake. But away from the conventions and inhibitions of English Victorian life he seems to have been able to drop his reserve and enjoy himself to the full. After a jovial dinner in New York he writes, "Much Madeira was drunk, much laughter was laughed, many jokes were joked". His son-in-law, in the official biography of Rosebery, makes the point perfectly clearly: "In most countries but most of all in America, the particular brand of shyness that puzzled many of his contemporaries did not affect his bearing either in the company of his intimate acquaintances or among strangers".[1] Curiously enough he showed the same rather unexpected absence of reserve when speaking at public meetings in his political heyday. The present writer remembers a veteran from the East Riding of Yorkshire describing Rosebery at a meeting at Leeds Town Hall at the beginning of this century. Rosebery's voice was not especially powerful and the building was packed from floor to ceiling; some heckling broke out which the superficial observer might have been forgiven for supposing would completely quell the reserved aristocrat. On the contrary, Rosebery threw back quip for quip and jibe for jibe so that he entranced and dominated that great meeting. The explanation for this is—and it is also part of the explanation of the charm of his journal—that he was one who understood human nature and knew how to bring out the best in it. Readers of this book will be deeply grateful to Mr Antony Grant for laying before them this gay and sparkling sketch of the New World in which, against a background of places and events brilliantly described, the chance acquaintances of travel assume reality and spring to life.

1. The Marquis of Crewe, K.G.: *Lord Rosebery*; London, John Murray, 1931.

Part One

Introduction

ARCHIBALD PHILIP PRIMROSE (1847–1929) succeeded his grandfather as fifth Earl of Rosebery in 1868. He was two when his
father died, and was brought up by his mother, sister of the historian
Lord Stanhope, and closely connected to the two Prime Ministers
Pitt. His mother's family was noted for its intellect, his father's
for a touch of eccentricity, while his step-father, last Duke of
Cleveland, personified the lineage and boundless acres of Whig-
gery to which Rosebery belonged.

At home Lord Rosebery had country and town houses, racing
stables, an eminent position in society. In this same year Gladstone
nominated him Lord Lieutenant of Linlithgow, and the year before
Rosebery had refused a junior ministership.

He carried to the new world introductions, but in the old he left
behind the aura of privilege which glowed about the person of
noblemen.

Rosebery arrived less than a month after Black Friday on the
New York stock exchange. He did not tour the South, that was to
be visited next year, but he toured the prisons, the lunatic asylums,
the "hells" and tenements, conscientious as a man-about-town and
as a Liberal interested in social questions to see above and below
stairs.

The foreign policy of Secretary Hamilton Fish was cautious,
suitably enough in the aftermath of the Rebellion, as Rosebery
terms it. The Treaty of Washington in 1871 had submitted out-
standing differences between the United States and Great Britain

to an arbitration convention at Geneva. In the same way another potentially warlike situation, the *Virginius* affair, had been averted by diplomatic activity. In 1868 the Ten Years' War between Spain and Liberals in her colony of Cuba had broken out. The *Virginius*, buccaneering for the Liberals but sailing under the Stars and Stripes, was captured by the Spanish outside their territorial waters on October 31st, 1873. Fifty-three seamen, including Americans, were executed, but in spite of this extreme provocation, the ship was surrendered to the United States on December 12th, and the crisis was over.

From New York Rosebery travelled to the Territory of Utah, luxuriously if rather primly, with his English tea, on the transcontinental line which had been completed in 1869. Mormon relations with the Federal Government had been stormy, and the American Army had come first to besiege, then to stay encamped as a sort of garrison outside Salt Lake City. It was not until the Mormon Church accepted the President's manifesto prohibiting plural marriages, in 1890, that the condition of suppressed hostility was abated.

In Canada Rosebery stayed more conventionally with the Governor-General, the 3rd Lord Dufferin, later Viceroy of India and Marquess. During 1873 *The Times* had been regaling its readers in London with accounts of the Canadian Pacific scandal, so that Rosebery reached Ottawa with a considerable prejudice against the government of Sir John Macdonald. Before reading his account it is as well to recollect that although Sir John went into eclipse for two years, he had another period of premiership starting in 1878 which only ended at his death in 1891.

Before launching into the more limpid stream of Lord Rosebery's own narrative the reader may require something about his later life. In 1878 he married Hannah, only daughter of Baron Mayer Amschel de Rothschild; they had four children.

Rosebery entered Gladstone's second administration as Under-Secretary for the Home Department, 1881–83; Lord Privy Seal and Commissioner of Works, 1885. He was Foreign Secretary in Gladstone's brief third administration, 1886, and again in his last

government, 1892–94. On Gladstone's retirement in 1894, Rosebery was Prime Minister for sixteen months.

Lady Rosebery died in 1890 and without her support and
encouragement the difficulties of leading the Liberal Government
from the House of Lords, with an uncongenial leader of the
Commons, together with his own hypersentitive temperament,
made prolonged political success impossible.

A.R.C.G.

Editor's Note

LORD ROSEBERY left the Durdans, Epsom, "his real home",[1] to his elder daughter, Lady Sybil Grant, for her lifetime. Her son, C. R. A. Grant, my father, inherited the residue of the contents on her death. This included an old and shabby suitcase of unusual shape, found in the library, containing notebooks, corrected proofs and similar literary paraphernalia, among them this journal. My father asked me to prepare it for publication.

It seemed best and in the interests of readability to present the text as far as possible unaltered, with the minimum of footnotes. Nothing has been omitted. Insertions, *marked with square brackets*, have been made where Rosebery seems to have left out a word necessary to the sense. *Round brackets with an asterisk* have been used to indicate later marginal notes by Rosebery himself.

Acknowledgements are due to my father, for his essential part in this publication and for his encouragement, and to my step-sister Caroline Combe, who typed the manuscript and helped in other invaluable ways. I have to thank Miss Romana Javitz, Curator of the Picture Collection, The New York Public Library, for finding almost all the illustrations. Mr A. S. Bell, of the National Library of Scotland Manuscripts Department, has been more than helpful in finding and selecting the material for the Appendix.

I acknowledge permission given by the Trustees of the National Library of Scotland to reproduce documents from the Rosebery

1. Robert Rhodes James: *Rosebery; a biography of Archibald Philip fifth Earl of Rosebery;* London, Weidenfeld and Nicolson, 1963; p. 55.

papers presented by Lord Primrose, to whom my gratitude is also due for their use.

I have to thank the Longfellow Trust, Longfellow House, Cambridge, Massachusetts, for permission to print Longfellow's letter and poem in this book.

A.R.C.G.

Calendar 1873

Part Two

I.   OPENING PAGE OF THE JOURNAL

The Journal

Oct 1. 1873

BREVOORT HOUSE, Fifth Avenue, corner of Eighth
Street, New York.

I copy the above address conscientiously to make quite sure that
I am where I am and that it is not all a dream. Yes, I am assuredly
in New York, having arrived yesterday morning at half past nine.

And first of the voyage. I left London on the night of Saturday
Sept 19 and crossed to Dublin. This was my third night of railway,
as on the two previous nights I had been employed in going and
coming from Scotland. All went off well on this third night except
that I slept but little, and that a bottle of champagne burst in my
bag thereby swamping de Tocqueville's first volume on America
and other illustrious books.

At Dublin I met Hurlbert and Cork. Cork was going to visit his
property. At Queenstown which we reached at two we embarked
at once on board a tug which took us on board the good steamer
'Russia'. The 'Russia' is supposed to be the fastest of the Cunard
ships.

Here I was introduced to Mr Duncan and his family, with whom
I afterwards lived on board. They consist of

Mr and Mrs Duncan (who was a Miss Sargent and whose
father was murdered during the Rebellion).
Miss Adele Duncan Mr Duncan's sister 24 years younger
than himself.

Miss Jessie Duncan Mr Duncan's daughter of 18, just 'out'.

Aleck Duncan the son a boy of 13, at Eton

Miss May Duncan at 12, with her nice German Governess

Fraulein Halsch or some such name

Dr John Metcalfe family physician and friend, and

Mr Hurlbert a leading American Journalist connected with the New York 'World', formed with myself the rest of the party

Hurlbert and I shared the 3rd and 4th officer's room—a capital deck cabin.

The weather was fine throughout the whole voyage, except that on Thursday night it came on to blow, and on Friday morning blew a gale (a sailor's not a landsman's gale) from the North East. However I was rather glad as I was perfectly well and had the experience of a real 'gale of wind'. Moreover the light on Friday morning was beautiful beyond compare: the huge waves, blue as heaven, with the sun glancing upon them, chafing about as if irresolute what to destroy, sometimes towering high with white crests like the Alps and sometimes hurrying frantically forward as if the Queen of Beauty had been seen in the South West. Then a great monster would throw us down into the trough of the sea as if impatient of our presumption in facing the ocean and tower behind us with the petrels rollicking about over the brilliant blue and white. The indecision of the sea was caused by the struggle between the North East wind and the Gulf Stream.

On the Thursday we had another sensation due to the Gulf Stream, and that was a flying fish which was good natured enough to come on board, and be caught. It is blue with a flat snaky head, and as like a swallow as a fish can well be.

On the Sunday and Monday Sept 28 and 29 we had such lovely weather that it made many of us regret having to leave the ship. Nevertheless at 6 on the Tuesday morning I was up and agog to see land. We had vainly waited all Monday to see a pilot boat, and as this anxiety may appear excessive to landsmen I will explain the reason, which is that the pilot boat is the subject of innumerable bets and lotteries. There are 24 numbered pilot boats and 1 £ lotteries of 24 people are formed each of whom have a number. The number corresponding to the pilot boat the ship takes wins. There were only two lotteries, and I who have never been near winning a lottery was sagacious enough to be in both. I drew 3 in one and 23 in the other, but the winning number was 4. Moreover I had bets as to the number being odd which I lost. And I betted that the pilot put his left foot on board first, which I won: and that he had an odd number of children which I won: and that he was born on an odd day of the month which I lost. So when the steamer stopped to take the pilot on board, it may be imagined what a rush there was of human beings in various dresses and undresses to see his number and his first foot, and his hat (the colour and size of which are betted upon).

It was a dull morning, but nothing could spoil the beauty of the two noble days as we steamed past Fort Lafayette, Fort Tomkins, Fort Hamilton and Staten Island.

There is not much to say of the other passengers. They were 211 in number, the passengers, and almost all American. There was the beauty of the ship Miss Keck the eldest daughter of a Cincinnati merchant, travelling with Mr and Mrs Cunningham also of the porcine city. Then the Misses Van Veghten, secondary and somewhat jealous beauties travelling with their father and brother. Then a parson of 6 ft 4 inches with a virgin sister of equal size named McVicar: he gave us a sermon on the Sunday. Then there were two lieutenants who sat next to me and scowled at the other passengers. They always addressed each other as "lew-tennent", and punctiliously saluted each other when they met. They also stated to their friends among the passengers that they were always mistaken for English gentlemen (by the bye they did not say 'mis'), which compliment I hereby gratefully acknowledge on behalf of my country. Then there was Mr Seyton a New York banker, and Dr Barker a New York Physician with practice and without voice; and one or two Englishmen, Geiger and Heyder and Easton. The latter was a squire of all the young ladies, to whom he introduced himself, but there was a slight coolness on his suddenly announcing during the last day that he had a wife and family in Virginia. Then there was a man whom the young ladies vowed was 'real sweet', and whom made great play with Miss Keck, and a gigantic Miss Thomas from Baltimore. I have written down enough names now, so will only add that our somewhat misanthropic Captain's name was Cook, and the doctor's name (the name of a very pleasant good fellow) Wallace.

The time passed very quickly, what with reading my wine-sodden copy of de Tocqueville, and what with romping with Prescott, a little grandson of the historian's whom we called "the little Hero" and, last not least, with eating and drinking. For there were five meals for those who could eat them. There was breakfast at 9.30, and luncheon at 12, and dinner at 4 and supper at 9.30. The staple food was Pork and Beans, a famous New England dish, with broiled sardines for supper.

Here I will leave a space for our daily runs, which I hope to get from Miss Duncan, and about which there were daily lotteries.

at noon		
Sept 22	..	290
Sept 23	..	343
Sept 24	..	338
Sept 25	..	347
Sept 26	..	301
Sept 27	..	336
Sept 28	..	335
Sept 29	..	323

Sept 30.

On arriving I waited for Hurlbert to get his luggage which took 2½ hours. The Custom House is strict and corrupt: the appearance of Cato and the reality of Verres:

We land in Jersey city, then drive into a ferry boat, like a section of a street, which takes us to New York. I went to the Brevoort

House, where I got a capital sitting room bed room and bathroom, no 35.

My luggage not coming, Geiger (who is also here) and I walked up and down Broadway all the afternoon. The same reason compelled me to give up dining with Hurlbert at the Manhattan Club, and to dine en-famille with the Duncans who excused my ship clothes. After dinner Duncan took me to the Union Club where he was warmly received and the Manhattan Club where there was nobody, at both of which clubs I was admitted a visitor. We also went to see the Fifth Avenue Hotel a huge town of an inn.

The commercial panic here has been the greatest ever known. Wall Street was a compact mass of eager furious heads, and the police had to drive waggons up and down to prevent a mob. As the news kept coming in of fresh disasters men fell down on the floor of the Stock Exchange in fits. When it was announced that it had been decided to close the Exchange for a week poor wretches went almost mad. One significant sign of the agony was that in the crack club—the Union—fifty dollars more were taken at the bar for drinks than had ever been known before in one evening.

Duncan and his partner Sherman both of whom were in the ship had a terribly anxious time (*and a very narrow squeak. They succumbed the next year I think) as when they left England the crisis had only just begun.

Oct 1.

This morning I woke early. Geiger and I breakfasted together at 8.

In the New York Herald of this morning I see a long paragraph detailing an 'interview' with me—the able production of a man who came and talked to me in the hall of the hotel. Thank Heavens, I did not answer many of his questions, or I should have been put in a very ridiculous light.

I never saw such a day—a day to dream of and to rave of: clear, bright, with a heavenly cheerfulness in the sky and a mad vivacity in the air. No one can wonder at the vitality or self confidence of the Americans who has breathed their October air: ruin and discomfiture are or seem mere trifles, and misfortunes have no more power than water on a duck's back. I felt as if in all justice I ought to break my leg or suffer some awful accident in order to handicap my health.

I walked to Wall Street and visited Duncan at his office. In all these American offices there is a ceaseless little instrument ticking away and stamping with apparent petulance on a long piece of tape: but its mimic anger is explained when one sees the tape slowly unrolling itself printed with the latest stock quotations from every part of the world.

Duncan and I walked down Wall Street and went to the brokers' luncheon place in Pine Street, where many men are seen employed in opening oysters—one of the dreariest occupations in the world unless one should find a pearl, I fancy—and handing them one by one to the consumer. At the other end of the bar one has ones' drink when one has finished one's oysters.

I met Geiger and we walked right back to the Brevoort House & thence to the Fifth Avenue Hotel where we picked up Easton and Heyder. Thence in a street car to the Central Park, which is by far the finest public park I have ever seen in variety of scenery. After walking there we walked home by Mr Stewart's marble palace and the gigantic Windsor Hotel and the synagogue with a crowd of Hebrews waiting outside its closed doors till they should open, for it is the feast of the Atonement.

I dined with Mr Ward at the Manhattan Club. How am I to describe him? Hurlbert said to me of a German merchant that he was a great client of our host. "But" says I "you told me he was a general in the Army?" "So he was" replied Hurlbert "before the war: now he is one of our leading barristers".

The feast was in honour of a soft shell turtle, a beast only found in two rivers in Alabama, and now made into soup. It is excessively rare and one had not been seen in New York for four years. Moreover we had a rather coarse fish called Sheepshead, some green indian corn (or 'corn' simply as it is called here) and Carolina rice-birds, which are the same as the reedbirds of the North.

We waited half an hour for Mr Evarts (who was the American counsel in the Geneva arbitration), who came at last. Dinner was nominally at 6. Besides Mr Evarts there was General Lorton a distinguished Confederate officer, Charles O'Connor the leading American barrister, Mr Cranstoun, and others, whom I do not remember except Hurlbert between whom and Mr Evarts I sat. There was also Judge Curtis.

Mr Evarts talked a little too much and somewhat too much about himself: but this is the only shadow of reproach that could be made for he and all were very agreeable. He told us that one night he was closeted till 11 with President Johnson advising him about his impeachment and from 11 to 1 consulting with other law officers on the impeachment of President Davis: a sufficiently curious experience.

At this dinner many met of the North and South who had not met for years. They were extremely good humoured together and talked about the war as a matter of history telling anecdotes of their experiences.

Afterwards I walked home with Evarts who gave me a lecture on England and America ending with a peroration in the most approved style. Then I joined Easton, Heyder, Geiger and a Scotch friend of Geiger's called McEwen, in a walk.

I bought a tall hat and wideawake today—cost me seventeen dollars—but then the shopman said I had a Daniel Webster forehead, so I could not cavil about price!

Oct 2.

Easton, Geiger and I breakfasted together. Afterwards I explored Appleton's for books and noted many which I should like to buy on my return.

Then I returned home and wrote. At 3 the same men and I drove in a hired carriage round the Central Park, and walked in it. We were twice run away with, and the whole business was rather reckless.

I dined with Geiger in the hotel to meet Mr Huntington who originated the charges against Sir John Macdonald. There were also present McEwen, Heyder, Mr Seyton who was in the 'Russia', Mr Thompson. Afterwards I had a long conversation with Mr Huntington, who was very full and goodnatured in his explanations. Afterwards again McEwen and Geiger took me to a supper, which I cannot describe, as I have forsworn the word 'bored'.

Oct 3.

Easton, Geiger and I breakfasted at 9.30 this morning. Heyder joined us, and we walked out together. Hurlbert and Duncan came: then Mr Huntington: and he and I walked about the street for fully an hour while he expounded to me this Pacific railway Scandal. Then he took me to his hotel and gave me a glass of Catawba wine—a native production.

I lunched with the Duncans, where were Miss Cunard and Miss Potter. I afterwards drove to 'the Tombs' to see that famous prison, but was too late, and must go another day. Afterwards I walked about the Streets till Nature gave way and my feet were entirely exhausted. The air here is so buoyant that one walks till one drops.

Allen formerly of Joynes' [house at Eton] came to see me, which was very friendly. I dined at the Duncan's—a Mr Cadwallader a barrister the only stranger. Thence to the opera where Nilsson Capoul and Miss Cary sang in 'Faust'. I don't know what has come to Nilsson, she has lost voice and face. I was introduced to Miss Penniman and Mrs Cutting two good looking women. Then Miss Stevens was there, the great beauty and heiress, and Miss Consuelo Ysnaga the beauty.

The opera house is a fine building with good acoustic property. It belongs to a company (of which Mr Duncan is one) who derive little or no income from the opera, but £60,000 a year by letting it out to public meetings (which pay from £50 to £100) and balls

II. MENDACIOUS CLUB
(*left to right*) Sam Ward, Rosebery, W. H. Hurlbert

(A). JOHN TAYLOR
One of the twelve apostles

(B). BRIGHAM YOUNG
Mormon president

(C). PATRICK SHEA

(D). ROSEBERY

III.

(which pay from £100 to £150 including lights and I think attendance).

Saturday Oct 4.

Today I breakfasted with Mr Sam. Ward a great character and lobbyist—a lobbyist is the deus ex machina of American politics; and Hurlbert in the hotel. Afterwards we three with Geiger drove to the Jerôme Park Races—about ten miles from New York. It is a pretty course with commodious stands: but the "track" as they call it is of light friable earth in which the horses are plunged up to their fetlocks and which covers the Spectator with dust. Everything is unlike our English races. Horses are being galloped up and down the course except when the races are going on, as a horse is not considered to be fit to start for a race unless he is warm from a gallop of two or three miles in deep ground under a hot sun. The little negro jockeys are also extraordinary as the shape of their head prevents a cap remaining on it when the horse begins to move. If a horse pulls, they clasp their legs round its neck till their feet meet. I was in the timekeepers' stand with two silent men holding watches, and there was nothing round us but excited negro helpers and grooms who screamed and laughed deliriously during the race. Prior the English trainer now trainer to Mr Belmont was there as well as two English Jockeys whose names I will insert when I remember them. The names were Evans and Barbee.

It was not a very eventful day and writing about it as I do on the evening of my arrival at Salt Lake I feel that it is not worth dwelling upon, except as regards the geniality of the Americans. I was introduced to all sorts of people from Senator Bayard to John Morrissey, ex representative pugilist and hell keeper: I am not sure by the bye that the last capacity is 'ex'. Sam Ward had a sporting friend called 'King' Valentine who was supposed to be likely to be offended if we do not follow his tips, so we each had ten dollars worth of tickets at the pari mutuel on the first two races: as one horse was dead lame and the other started two hundred yards

2

behind the rest, I made up my mind that is was better to forfeit
Mr Valentine's esteem and give up buying tickets. Sam Ward
however had not the courage to take this course and continued
losing. The once famous horse Harry Bassett whose owner
challenged the world with him ran in one race, but was only I
think 'out for an airing'.

The president and two vice presidents acted as Judges. Their
box is high up and they appear to judge by a tape run from the
winning post to their box over the horses' heads. August Belmont
is the president and Duncan is one of the vice presidents of whom
there are five or six.

There was one coach and four on the ground with two pretty
girls (at least) upon it—Miss Consuelo Ysnaga and Miss Gandy.
The Duncans were also there and Mrs Penniman. Although they
took the largest sum in gatemoney ever known at this meeting
(5000 dollars) this was due to the large quiet crowd of men in the
stand not to any great show of ladies.

All our party dined with the Duncans as well as Balfour. I did not
like dining there two days running, and said I should not, but
was overruled by Ward and Hurlbert who said I evidently did
not understand American hospitality. No more I do, for it is
illimitable.

Sunday Oct 5. New York.

Geiger and I breakfasted together. Afterwards I went to church
with the Duncans to Grace church. And I was rewarded for the
singing was very good—many of the hymns original and striking
—and the address delivered instead of a sermon, as it was Communion Sunday, quite admirable. It was preached by the rector
Dr Potter, its occasion was the Collect of the day (the 17th Sunday
after Trinity), and the subject was the love of position and putting
oneself forward—as great said the parson if not greater in the New
world than the Old. He told us that he had thanked John Stuart

Mill for his defence of American institutions in England, and that Mill had done nothing but blush, almost painfully, in reply. Coming out of church I was shewn Mr Astor, a hard dreary looking old man and the richest in the world.

In the afternoon the Duncans took me over to their villa in Staten Island. It was a lovely day and the views were divine—New York though so near appearing distinct but as it were inanimate and floating in the haze like an enchanted city. Nothing can give an idea of the pellucid rapture of the atmosphere.

Sam Ward gave Hurlbert, Geiger and myself a dinner at the Brunswick Restaurant. It was pleasant and cheery. But imagine my astonishment at seeing the grim Governor of the Tombs come and sit at the adjoining table with a pretty young woman whom he was a courting. I would if I were a pretty young woman, as soon be courted by a rusty padlock.

Sam was in great form and was as usual hailed with delight by the waiters who all had some sly little memories to compare with him.

Monday Oct 6. New York—cold and rainy in the afternoon.

I went to breakfast with Hurlbert at the Manhattan Club—where was the late Democratic Mayor of New York Oakey Hall. After breakfast the latter and I set out for the Courts of Law over which he shewed me thoroughly, and which were quite impressive enough it seemed to me though the Judges did not cover their heads with horsehair or their bodies with gowns. I was introduced to a good many judges, notably Judge Blake who is for political reasons a sort of Fenian Head Centre, and Chief Justice Daly who kept a juror waiting in front of him a quarter of an hour while he discoursed to me on the meteorology of America. This strikes me much—the absolute submission to recognised authority which seems socially to distinguish the Americans: but of course, in saying this, I have only slight data to go upon.

I went into Recorder Halkett's court where he was hearing a case of theft—a negro being the defendant for whose character Mr Cutting was there to speak. The prosecution was conducted by the Public Prosecutor i.e. the 'district Attorney' or one of his deputies. We asked him if the case would last long. "No" he said "the fact is—after hearing the evidence I do not think the man is guilty". Then two or three witnesses for character were examined, the prisoner himself was sworn and gave his account of the matter (this I believe is a novelty even here) and after a few words from the Recorder, the Jury found the man 'Not Guilty'. Hall told me that when he was public prosecutor, he always stopped the case whenever convinced of the defendant's innocence—this was one of the advantages of having a public prosecutor.

The prisoner sat on the foremost bench in the crowd, but there were no policemen visible (they were posted at the doors) and the other prisoners came in alone. This was striking.

I afterwards saw the register books of real property and mortgages. In the latter by a simple index one can at once see the number and extent of one's dearest friend's mortgages. How popular this institution would be in England.

Then we saw the American Doctors' Commons, the volumes where a copy of every will is kept. Two we were shown were curious:—one was Major André's, the other that of Gouverneur Morris, who makes provision for the education of his son in some place of learning—so long as it is not in the state of Connecticut 'the craft and mean cunning of whose inhabitants though sometimes attempted to be hid under a veil of hypocrisy and deceit is too well known to be particularized'—or some such words.

We then went on to the Tombs the great prison here. It is an intensely dreary looking building, as is meet, of a sort of Egyptian architecture. The Governor shewed us over. The cell of Stokes—the murderer of Fisk was shut up. His cause had been for trial that morning—but he had pleaded indisposition and it had been deferred till the day after tomorrow. But presently a negro lad was shown in. I asked who it was. "One of Stokes' servants". It seemed so strange that this man who will probably be condemned to death this week or next should have his establishment like other folks. I wonder what they say of him in his servants' hall. I peeped in, so that he could not see me, and saw him in bed trying medicines:— a common type of American predatory face.

The rest of the afternoon was so rainy that I remained indoors. I dined with Balfour at the Travellers' Club, meeting Romilly. The latter and I afterwards went to the Opera, where 'Lucia': I to the box of the Duncans who took me home. Duncan introduced me to Miss Ysnaga and to Colonel Jerôme Bonaparte—a son or grandson of Jerôme's by his American marriage.

Balfour and Romilly afterwards took me to a hell— Watson's —which I much wished to see. We were at once admitted and given supper. We afterwards played at roulette a little to say we had done it. I won 50 dollars.

Tuesday Oct 7. New York—very cold.

This morning Hurlbert breakfasted with Geiger and me at the Brevoort House: I afterwards to get money in Wall Street and a ticket to Salt Lake. Afterwards to take luncheon with the Duncans and say good bye.

Geiger gave a farewell feast in my honour to Hurlbert, Ward and myself at the Brevoort House. Afterwards they (except Ward) saw me to the train. Here Parker joined me as he is going as far as North Platte with me.

Geiger had got me a letter from General Porter, Vice President of the Pullman car company, recommending me to its agents and conductors, which was wonderfully useful. The conductor now made the smoking room over to us instead of a section so that we were wonderfully comfortable. The beds are just like cabin berths only much wider.

The train is generally composed of different Pullman cars (with of course the ordinary cars): one is arranged as a drawing room with a harmonium, another with two private drawing rooms and so on.

Wednesday Oct 8. In the cars

I slept capitally and was up early to see a lovely morning and breakfast at Syracuse which was the first time I had seen Americans in the frenzy of eating. They appear to eat not for luxurious enjoyment but simply to make "the 'tomach 'tiff'" as the Hottentot says: and very stiff it must sometimes be. I soon fell into the way of it, and could finish my dinner in three minutes and enjoy the spare twenty two on the platform as well as anybody. I have not gained any agility with my knife, but intend practising in private. In the middle of this lovely day we got to Niagara and walked across the Suspension bridge admiring the lovely scenery and the glimpse of the cataract. Afterwards, a hotel car having been added, we dined in our smoking room as luxuriously as we could in New York.

I have by the bye omitted to mention the Hudson, whose stream we saw dimly for some miles after leaving New York, the falls of Rochester which we traversed this morning, and the extraordinary graduated system of locks at Lockport. After Niagara we passed into Canada and a quantity of wild rather dreary backwood scenery: except the country for some miles beyond Hamilton which is charming. Here we passed a little country trotting meeting, with its small crowd and its trotters preparing to start all of which looked very quaint and pretty.

At Detroit or rather Windsor on the Canadian bank the train passed bodily into a great steamboat which carried us over to Detroit on the American bank of Detroit river. After this it being late at night I know nothing, but I presume we returned to the scenery of the morning—the bright comfortable wooden houses and the spare stems of Indian corn looking like crazy fluttering ghosts discovered suddenly by the daylight, and on the ground the golden pumpkins basking jovially in the sun—like a farm of the Hesperides.

Thursday Oct 9. A lovely day, very hot.

Next morning however we reached Chicago—the 'garden city' and pride of the West. It was an eventful day for it was the second anniversary of the fire, and the town was preparing to rejoice. And well it might for the fire has been a second Augustus—it found the city wooden and left it brick, stone and marble. Certainly it is inconceivable how quickly all has been built.

Parker and I breakfasted at the Sherman House and then we parted for a time: as he goes to Omaha by the Chicago Burlington and Quincey line and I by the Chicago and North Western. Here also I parted with my dear cheery conductor Page.

I got a drawing room in the car with a very taciturn conductor. He however told me that he had helped to build the first hut in Denver. He also said that law was as much respected in these out of the way regions as in New York and that justice was more impartially administered. Just outside Chicago I met a train in which I saw the Duke of Manchester's head, but there was not time to get down and speak to him.

We crossed the Mississipi today at Fulton, where there is a very fine bridge. The trains go very slowly over these bridges and the bridges creak a good deal while one can see nothing below one but a few beams and the river, so that one has to get accustomed to them before one feels quite safe. The river is of immense breadth but seemed exceedingly low in its banks. It was oppressively hot all day.

Oct 10. Fine day.

This morning we came into a more wooded and uneven "bluff" country. Here I was tormented by the sight of countless prairie chickens, so like grouse that it was extremely tantalizing. We crossed the Missouri on a very long bridge, but it is disappointing inasmuch as it is the muddiest river I ever saw: the breadth and expanse is very great, but it is very shallow just now. It here divides Iowa from Nebraska, Council Bluffs being the Iowan city and Omaha the Nebraskan. As they are practically one city, it is needless to say they are the bitterest possible enemies, and the result is that we were changed at Council Bluffs into a train which was merely to take us across the bridge—a process which took an hour. At Omaha Parker's train was late so I made an excursion into the town. I was attracted to a driver who was being chaffed by an American. "You're a nice sort of chap, you are" said the American "A Scan-hoofian—you are". "Scanhoofian" screamed the driver a long lad of sixteen or so "Scanhoofian a nice sort of a feller *you* are to be coming and talking—you don't even know the name. Well, I'll tell you, I'm a Scandinavian—now tell me all *you* know about the Scandinavians". The American was overwhelmed by the Dane: and I therefore hired the Dane's carriage as a reward. I took with me a new friend a young Chicago bagman who was very pleasant. He asked me everything about myself—some questions which made me rather shamefaced—what my occupation was and how I earned my living. He would not believe I was 26 which I can well understand, for though he was not 20 he had seen much more of life than I had. He had been to England and to the African diamond fields: and now he was traveller for an icehouse—I mean a house dealing in ice—at a handsome salary. I stopped to be shaved, and the barber asked me several questions one of which was " Well I don't suppose you've got such a barber's shop as *this* in England". I meekly evaded the question by saying that he certainly was a much better shaver than the English barbers. I was long in the place and when I came out I apologised to the Chicagoan. "Oh" he said "never mind I went and got three orders for 'ice' while you were in there".

The town like most new American towns has roads made with a view to the traffic of two million inhabitants. The houses are wood, and the names betray the presence of many 'Scanhoofians' and Germans. There is an excellent hotel. High above the town is a very handsome building with a tower. It is the finest building I have seen in these parts, and shews the difference between the new and the old world. In the old world it would be or would have been the keep of some feudal prince or the refuge and fortress of some despotic king. Here it is the Schoolhouse.

At last Parker arrived and we set off. We now passed through a great agricultural country or rather a country of great agricultural possibilities. It is destined I suppose when England is only a country of pastures, market gardens and workshops to supply us with corn. Further on we passed into the prairie. Here as it grew evening the country was lit up by fires, one a line of dancing flames more than a mile long was very grand: and the smoke of distant fires looked sometimes like a distant view of Newcastle.

At Schuyler (Nebraska) a new sensation. Some Pawnees from a station in the neighbourhood appeared. Everyone was excited at this first view of the proud native savage: and a more dirty repulsive bestial fellow creature than the proud native savage I have seldom or never seen except perhaps on the outskirts of a racecourse. Near here there is a much more important and desirable colony—from Nova Scotia. However the Pawnees now that game is scarce are making their livelihood by raising fair crops.

At North Platte at 1 o'clock or 3 o'clock next morning I am not sure which Parker left me. These are his happy hunting grounds, where Lord and Lady Dunraven are waiting for him. I must say it is rather enviable, and the prairie grouse are so numerous!

Oct 11. Fine—a cold morning.

Today we were on a great waste of land all the morning, seeing a good many antelope and those dear little chaps—the prairie dogs who are like Mark Tapley[1] jolly under the greatest difficulties.

We breakfasted at Sidney, where there are great flocks of sheep, and dined at Cheyenne. Here I saw a figure that I felt sure I knew. It was Bertie Mitford. We parted at luncheon in the St James' Club nine or ten months ago, and we met at Cheyenne in the Territory of Wyoming in the Western States of America. He was bent

---

1. See Charles Dickens: *Martin Chuzzlewit.*

2*

homewards, and we only had a few minutes to talk as his train was going.

After this, constant wooden sheds, meant to protect the line against snow showed that we were getting up into the hills, and the more we ascended the more deliciously bracing and clear was the air. Sherman (8,235 feet above the sea) was our highest point and claims to be the loftiest railway station in the world. After this the descent became rapid and we looked on great undulating lines of little hills more like Atlantic waves than any earthly formation— When "the little hills skip like rams", this country will be just like a sea in a storm.

Sunday Oct 12. Fine & warm.

Today we gradually approached some very fine scenery. We breakfasted at Greenriver—a little hell of monte men and universal swindlers: one of our passengers having a ten dollar note snatched out of his hand in the little timber saloon. A worse danger is that of losing one's train, for these decoys wear false tickets in their hats like real travellers, and invite them to come into a saloon saying that they are also passengers and know that the train is not going for ten minutes at least. We dined at Evanston in Utah, where I met Skelmersdale: on his way home.

All today the country seemed inhabited chiefly by Chinese. Our breakfast was cooked by them and they waited on us at dinner. They are very good waiters—neat quick quiet and anxious to do well. They are very industrious also, but weak. Their dress is a sort of long white blouse reaching the knees or lower and loose white pantaloons: this with the plait of hair wound round their heads makes them look like Bloomers, if there be such things now.

At last we entered the great canyons or ravines which lead from the entrance of Utah territory to Ogden. It is impossible to give any notion of their variety and abruptness. The railroad winds along the bottom while on each side the mountains rise to the height of a thousand feet. One of the finest passes is called the Devil's

Gate. Then there is a very curious sort of natural groove of rocks which is called the Devil's Slide. Then there is the Pulpit rock which is of a quaint topheavy shape. Some of these hills are crowned with little walls to shelter riflemen and with rocks prepared to roll down upon assailants: all the work of the Mormons when threatened by President Buchanan's army in 1859.

As the train approaches nearer Salt Lake or rather Ogden the scenery becomes more and more beautiful: and when at last we broke from out of the ravines to approach the plain on which Ogden is situated, one could form some idea of the feelings of the Mormons after their great march. It must have been a solemn moment, when, after toiling through the majestic canyons—some with great sandstone boulders like red fortresses of nature some bare and repulsive, they came to these last hills, (if they were as I saw them) rosy in the sun, but radiant with a hundred natural hues, violet and russet and crimson and gold, and were told by the inspired voice that these were the gates of the land of promise.

Here we came to our first Mormon settlements. One would have remarked them at once, as, at the first station there were two pretty chubby English children offering plums and greengages for sale, with pleasant faces destitute of any expression.

At Ogden (the second Mormon city but sadly leavened with Gentiles and gamblers) we changed carriages, and, after waiting there for some time and a tedious journey of two hours we arrived at Salt Lake City about 9.30. I put up at the Walker House in Main Street, and after supper and a short stroll went to bed. Much struck by seeing a man kneel down and drink from the gutter at the side of the street.

Monday Oct 13.

WALKER HOUSE, Salt Lake City. Very hot.

After shaving and washing for an extraordinary time I breakfasted at 7. Soon after Captain Forbes to whom I had sent a letter of introduction from Sam Ward came in and we went out

together. He is here to look after the interests of the English share-
holders of the silver mines here. We walked first to the Zion
Mercantile Cooperative Institution (the motto of which stamped
on all its goods is "Holiness to the Lord") to find Mr Clawson the
president or superintendent to whom I had a letter of introduction.
Mr Clawson is short and very American in appearance with the
usual heavy moustache. He has married two of Brigham Young's
daughters, is an Apostle, theatre-manager, head of this great
cooperative institution and altogether a man of mark. Leaving him
we went to the Tabernacle over which we were shown by a
Wolverhampton man. It is a very wonderful building, with a roof
shaped like the long half of a cocoa-nut without a support, calculated to hold 13000 sitters with a magnificent organ made in the
city. The organ has 2100 pipes I think and 800 more to go in to
complete it. The large pipes are made of the native pinewood which
is supposed to give a very soft mellow tone. The organ is on a dais
at the end, and in front of it are the seats of the president apostles
and other dignitaries. Two large flags—stars and stripes are laid
over chairs—one on each side of these high seats. Across the roof
wires are drawn from one lateral wall to the other (*this to con-
trol and guide the sound), but, as a rule the acoustic properties are
said to be admirable. Our guide told us he had seen as many as
16000 people in the Tabernacle.

The design was very much the work of Brigham Young. This
Tabernacle is always to be used even when the new temple is
finished—the new temple being intended simply for certain high
functions, the tabernacle for ordinary use. In the tabernacle the
sexes are divided, the women taking the two inner divisions of
seats.

The new Temple or what there is of it is within a few yards of
the tabernacle. The walls are only at most three feet from the
ground. There were a good many men at work there, some I was
told, to work off their tithing to the Church, and some out of
piety. I am a little sceptical about the last.

I saw the sketch of what the new temple is to be—an imposing
structure with a good many towers. I innocently asked who the

architect? to which the man replied "the original design was by inspiration, Sir".

I gave ten dollars to the fund for the temple, as it is customary to give something. After this Elder Clawson took us to the Theatre— a pretty little building just done up in white and gold in the French style. Thence he took us to the editor's office of the 'Salt Lake Herald'. The editor was a stout intelligent looking man called Sloane. He had once passed by Skelmersdale's place, he said, when in England, during the coming of age rejoicings. This accounts for a paragraph in his paper of this morning which had puzzled me— "Lord Skelmersdale has just left this city. He is of Ormskirk, England, where he is beloved by a highspirited and intelligent tenantry": which after all is more accurate than the announcement in the San Francisco paper "Lord I. Kilmerding has left this town for his home—the chalk little island".

After this Forbes took me and introduced me to Gurdon another naval officer also here in connection with these mines. He and I took a carriage driven by 'John', an apostate Mormon, to the American camp, a dusty jolty journey of three miles. Here there were some pleasant looking officers called Jamar and Mumford and a birdseye view of Salt Lake: the camp being 480 feet above the city. Then we drove on to the entrance of the Emigration Cañon where there is a good view again, and then home. The heat was so great that I went in and wrote. I ventured out afterwards but the heat was so great again than I returned. Moreover the dust was so thick that one could not see a man the other side of the street.

I dined with Gurdon at the Townshend House. Forbes and another Englishman called Myers were there. After dinner Gurdon and I went to the play. We arrived at 7.30 punctually or a little before and remained without moving till 11.45. The mixture was curious and more especially when contrasted with the little spick and span French theatre. On one side was a Salt Lake Dandy with diamond studs and lavender gloves, with his young woman also smart and holding a fan she did not know how to hold. On the other side there was the mother of thirteen (to look at her) freely administering nature's founts to her baby, weeping copiously and laughing loudly whenever the play demanded. In the middle of the piece a man marched in with five wives in the midst of whom he sat sultanically, and again after him two miners in flannel shirts and long boots.

In front of me there was a pitiful romance which I watched instead of the play. There was a gentleman called Harrison a tin-smith with whom I had had a transaction about a teapot in the afternoon. ("I reckon I'm out of them". "When will you have some more?" "When I've made them".) Well, Harrison was seated in the stalls a smug Welshman or Briton. On his right was his hideous legitimate wife: beyond her was her hideous legitimate daughter. On his left was his newly married wife with a young baby at her breast. The fat spouse was smartly dressed and the hideous daughter was also smart, but the poor Hagar with her pleasant kindly rather plain face was very simply dressed with no ornament but her wedding ring. The Sarah and daughter had sent her to Coventry it was obvious and tittered and laughed away amazingly—old Abraham joining. The other poor thing sat glum and melancholy clasping and fondling her baby. Her husband occasionally turned to her, but only getting sad answers and looks gave it up, and at last I saw the young mother shedding such bitter tears over her baby and trying to hide them. Presently she got up and left the house. The stepdaughter had occasionally looked round at her as if to observe how she took her exclusion, but Sarah studiously kept her head turned away. It was quite clear that the good man had taken unto himself the handmaid, an offence which his former family visited upon her.

The play was long and dreary and Uncle Tom was intolerable. There was a dear little Eva a daughter of Elder Clawson's. She died in the second act in bed, with a chorus of household blacks singing a hymn and uncle Tom uttering a sort of religious soliloquy. In the third act St Clare dies on a sofa with a chorus of household blacks singing a hymn and uncle Tom uttering a religious soliloquy. In the last act Uncle Tom happily expires on a pallet uttering a religious soliloquy with a chorus of household blacks singing a hymn.

Uncle Tom's wig was the same colour as his shirt and as the whole effect was dark with nothing visible but a pair of rolling eyeballs, he looked like a hoarse and offensively-canting owl in an ivy bush.

The play, what with sensational slavedriver and uncle Tom's religious soliloquies, was a happy combination of a 'penny dreadful' and the Athanasian creed. The audience were very innocent, very orderly and very easily pleased. They shrieked with laughter and delight at every little disaster that befell the slavedrivers. But there was a terrific round of applause, when the old Quaker appeals to the memory of his dead wife before fighting the ragged pedlar; 'Sainted Maria' he said 'help me to kick out this damned Yankee', and I confess it struck me that it was said with marked intention and so received by the Mormons. At the end of the performance was the apotheosis of Eva, somewhat rudely represented, as the kneeling cherubs looked just like the little children in their nightgowns that always appear tumbled about in a pantomine.

Tuesday Oct 14.
WALKER HOUSE, Salt Lake City—cold.

I got up pretty early on this cold gray morning, and went to the 'Herald' office and to the Zion Cooperative store to find out about president Young's movements. It appears that he will not be back tonight, nor till tomorrow evening. I have therefore determined to follow him.

Now after the expedition is over I proceed to recollect and write it down. I got letters from Elder Clawson to Bishop Harrington at American Fork and Bishop Smoote at Provo.

I lunched at one at a restaurant on half a wild-duck with Gurdon and Forbes. Soon afterwards it began snowing. At 2.30 the train started and in about two hours it arrived at American Fork which is the furthest point of the railway. Here there was a sort of half open cart the driver of which offered to take me to Provo. So I closed with him as it saved me the trouble of presenting a letter to Bishop Harrington and him the trouble of getting me horses. There were two other passengers—one a leading citizen of Provo, the other a long lanky lad. The leading citizen sat on the box seat, I existed in the shape of the letter Z somewhere behind him, and the lanky lad sat further back still. The leading citizen having asked me my country and then whether I had come in the mining interest, was so astounded to hear that I had not that he spoke to me no more.

The cart was drawn by two wiry Indian horses or mares rather and the foal of one of them skipped round and round the cart. When it ceased so to skip we stopped peering into the darkness to see what had become of it. It must be understood that snow and sleet were falling thick, that it was pitch dark soon after we started, and that the roads were a succession of deep dry ditches varied by short stretches of deep sand. Over these trenches the cart creaked and groaned and staggered, and one felt each time that at the next ditch it would either break its back or jolt itself into a jelly.

One thing amused me. There was a house which I thought we never should pass, it seemed a sort of Will o the wisp. However when we did pass it, this was easily explained. It was moving to another part of the country drawn by a team of oxen.

Everything comes to an end, except an Irish grievance and an Oxford bill, and this drive was no exception. We dropped the leading citizen at his house. Then the question was where was I going to? "To the Bishop", said I. "Which?" said they. "The Bishop" said I this time with some dignity. "But there are five here" said the driver. So I had to strike a match and see who it was to whom my letter was directed: it was the Mayor Bishop Smoote. So to Smoote's house we drove where a pretty young woman told me that Smoote was at the Town Hall. The Town Hall was brilliantly lighted up and I could see a supper going on. Sending in the letter I waited some time. At last Mayor Smoote came out with my letter, welcomed me and introduced me "Mr Earl Rosebery—Mrs Jones Mr Earl Rosebery—Mrs ahem Jones again, Mr Earl Rosebery—Mrs ahem Jones again". So I went out, paid my driver and let him go. However I shouted after him to get my luggage to which he did not respond, and finding my 'luggage' outside the door I was satisfied. But the reason that he drove off so quickly was that he had—and probably still has—Mrs Duncan's rug with him.

Coming back softly I found a conclave examining my letter of introduction and debating upon my style and titles. As I came in the verdict was "he IS", and henceforward I was addressed familiarly as "Earl", and introduced as "the earl of—dear me sir I do not recall your name".

We that is the ladies—married and a nice looking Miss—— who superintends one of the branch cooperative stores—and I sat talking in the waiting room with a deputation of two bishops who were sent out to make conversation. Presently the door opened, there was general sort of stir, everybody stood up, an old gentleman in a great coat comforter and shocking bad hat advanced taking off the hat, with the two other elderly gentlemen behind him. This was Brigham Young followed immediately by George A. Smith second president and Historian of the Church, and Elder Taylor who was with Joseph Smith when he died and now a leading member of the Twelve Apostles.

Brigham Young is something like Lord Ravensworth only of a smaller make. His mouth is firm, rather underjawed, his eye blue, his speech soft and deliberate, his teeth openly false. He was not well but was courteous and dignified, shewing me great attention and politeness, treating his followers who paid him devout and anxious homage with coolness if not haughtiness. Below him, I should say, there is wonderful fellowship and democracy—what one would hope and suppose were the manners of the primitive Christians: but of him the whole flock stand in obvious awe not to say fear.

George A. Smith is a stout tall florid Englishman of the middle class deriving a fictitious importance from spectacles.

John Taylor is a pleasant kindly garrulous old Englishman from Liverpool. He was in the cell with Joseph Smith when Joseph Smith was murdered. He received four balls, but escaped while the assassins were occupied in putting Smith's semianimate body against a wall and firing at it. Joseph Q. Cannon followed if not at once at any rate almost at once. He is by far the most attractive Mormon dignitary I have ever seen. He has a bright and earnest eye and manner: knows much more of what is going on in the outer world then the other Mormons, and is consequently and also naturally much more of a man of the world than they are. He is a very charming companion, and though, as I have said, a man of the world he is obviously an earnest believer in Mormonism.

After some conversation I was taken to the supper whereof there was a second relay. I sat between two dignitaries of the church, but still there was an originality about the business. In the middle of our meal the shirtsleeved waiter gave my right hand neighbour a great bang upon the back with his hand, shouting "How are you doing, Joe, pretty well as usual? Have some pie, it's prime". My neighbour's face was a picture. The waiter was a Scotsman. (*But I think the waiters were those who had supped at the first meal). All this festival I may mention was in honour of the dedication of the Courthouse or Town Hall in which we were assembled, which ceremony had taken place today. All such buildings and I believe private houses are publicly dedicated with prayer. Moreover the dance to which we ascended after supper was begun and ended with prayer. "We like to associate everything" they said "even our little amusements with prayer: and you see we do try and amuse ourselves in this present life, even though it is only passing the time till that unspeakable happiness we shall have hereafter." They are fond of alluding to their certainty of immense happiness in a future state, dwelling on the certainty. There is always a grace before but I do not think I ever heard one after meals. Somebody says "Brother Blank will you ask a blessing", and brother blank in a tone of voice as if he was asking for potatoes or discussing eligible investments—colloquially in fact—says "Lord we thank thee that thou has brought us safely here etc. etc.": it is quite short and very sensible.

After supper we went up to the ballroom, where they had begun dancing. I did not dance but sat and looked on. All the dances were Square or 'cotillons' as they were called, and each figure was called out in a loud voice by a sort of master of the revels who stood apart and called the figures as his fancy dictated. The chief beauties were the two Misses Smoote daughters of Bishop Smoote, Miss Sharp daughter of Bishop Sharp (the chairman of the Utah Central Railway) and the Miss —— I was introduced to down stairs. Then in the midst of dancing a little man like a Jew fiddler 'Brother Maibin' came forward and sang a song about a fair, another about a man being frozen by ice creams, and another about 'Our Village' by Tom Hood. Moved to this by the general applause, a large brother with a bass voice now came forward and sang a somewhat dreary and tragical ballad. Soon after this we went to bed. I was introduced in the ballroom to a brilliant crowd of Bishops, Colonels and Judges. Everybody danced, old as well as young, and the president himself would have danced but for rheumatism, as he is very fond it of and dances well. He soon went to bed taking with him Amelia, to whom I was introduced. She is a pleasant shrewd looking woman of about forty. I was also introduced to Bishop Hunter the genial old patriarch of the church.

Bishop Smoote was full, so Bishop Miller took me in. He is a plain slow kindly man, who told me that the revelation of polygamy was as great a trial of faith to him as to his first wife.

I was glad to get to bed in a large room hung round with coloured female heads, some of them such as one sees on the top of a box of French prunes. The bolster was stuffed with some dry crackling stuff but I could not make out what it was. I slept the sleep of the just for nine or ten hours.

Wednesday Oct 15. Provo—cold raw and snowy.

This morning Elder Taylor came over to breakfast and we breakfasted alone together, Bishop Miller sitting by. Elder Taylor discoursed at great length on religion—and presently Hiram Woodruff or Wilford Woodruff I understood Hiram but now think it was Wilford—came in. Then Taylor, Woodruff and I got into Bishop Smoote's cart—driven by young Smoote—and splashed through the city which is grandly situated between the mountains and the lake. It contains 4000 inhabitants and is the third Mormon city, Ogden being the second. It is spread over an immense space of ground relatively to the population, as each house is surrounded by a quantity of ground. We drove to the woollen factory they have established here which is the largest building I have seen since Chicago. They are justly proud of it. It architecture and proximity to the snow clad hills brought Turin to my mind. We went carefully over the whole building which is filled with the newest kinds of machinery which the pleasant and intelligent foreman explained to us. There was an Indian girl working there and she was said to be one of the best workers there.

Afterwards we drove to the University, or as we should call it Dayschool. There were no children there but a strong smell of apples: the children had all gone home to their dinners. The building had originally been a theatre and was occasionally used for dancing, besides obviously at present being also a fruit cupboard.

Then we went into the Cooperative Store—or rather the principal one for there are two both agencies of the central Zion Store.

After this there was much fidgetting. The president had expressed fears that 2 pm was too late to start, that we had better start at 1.30: and if we should keep the president waiting! So we hurried back to Bishop Smoote's where there was to be dinner.

President Young has a pleasant villa opposite Bishop Smoote's house, where he comes for change of air. All the houses here are particularly bright clean and brilliant.

At Bishop Smoote's there was a good many of the leading people of last night's ball. The Salt Lakeites dined, and the others waited upon them. There was some native wine served of which almost everybody but myself took a glass.

After this I went and took leave of kindly Bishop Miller, and tried at the Courthouse to see if Mrs Duncan's rug had been restored there, which was needless trouble on my part; and then we all waited the best part of an hour for President Young. But the President had a bad cold and tarried. Meanwhile we all got into a series of the light country waggons (*buggies) which stood in single file outside. I was placed in the first with Elder Taylor, and Miss Sharp who seemed very popular. There were four or five carts behind us. At least the President and Amelia jumped into their waggon, and drove off with injunctions to our driver not to press too hardly on their heels lest we should pole the prophet, we all following in single file.

At last we arrived at the spot two or three miles beyond American Fork where the line ends for the present.

My way had been beguiled by Apostle Taylor telling me all the narrative of how Joseph and Hyrum Smith had been shot in Nauvoo when he was with them in the cell. He told it circumstantially but without the slightest sign of emotion, although it should have been to him much as the Crucifixion was to the Twelve Christian Apostles. Joseph Smith when he saw Hyrum Smith shot dead, came forward, and taking a small revolver from Taylor fired it several times into the mob. Then Taylor attempted to get out of the window but received four balls and fell back into the room and crept under the bed. Joseph Smith then tried to get out of the window but receiving several shots fell to the ground outside. The assassins seeing this hurried down stairs to join the crowd round Smith's body, and put the body up against the wall and fired at it. Meanwhile Taylor and Willard Richards who was mysteriously unhurt escaped. Few men have been so near death and lived.

He excused the suppression of the Gentile Journal which led to the riot by saying that they considered it came under the powers given them in their charter to suppress nuisances. He said he had no doubt from the direction of several of the balls fired into Joseph Smith's dungeon that they came from the United States Militia placed outside to protect the Mormon prisoners.

Well we arrived at the end of the line, and president Young dismounted from his cart with a red handkerchief tied under his chin like a bonnet and a hat over it. President George A. Smith had also a flaming bandana tied round his head in the same way. We remained on this open spot for nearly if not quite an hour, president Young returning to his waggon. At last the train appeared: and we all crowded into the welcome warmth of the private presidential car. Into a room at the end of this car the prophet and Amelia retired. I sat and talked with Joseph Cannon, who was however presently summoned with George A. Smith to see the president, whom they found with a good deal of fever and wandering in the head. It was seven before we got back to Salt Lake. I could not say good-bye to Young as he was too unwell but I said goodbye to Amelia instead and to all the kindhearted Mormons in the train. I then went off to buy relics of Salt Lake—an oxhide whip and the spurs they use, and two pairs of the gloves which the Mormon ladies make and sell with cuffs of beaver fur. Some of them have flowers embroidered on the back.

A Mr Lounsbery a friend of Balfour's came and introduced himself to me and walked out with Gurdon and myself. Then I said goodbye to them and went up to my room where I was visited by kind old Apostle Taylor who presented me with a French copy of the Book of Mormon issued under his directions, and one or two controversial pamphlets by himself.

I sat up writing some time and packing, but the heat of the stove was too oppressive to do much, and so I went to bed, reflecting with real regret that this was my last night in Salt Lake.

Thursday Oct 16. Very cold.

WALKER HOUSE, Salt Lake City.

I was called and got up at the genial hour of half past four. At five we started in the omnibus for the station, and at ten minutes to six we steamed off to Ogden. At Ogden there was a great struggle for the places in the Pullman cars wherein my former conductor had secured me a drawing room.

We breakfasted at Ogden and dined at Evanston. On this journey I produced one of my two packets of tea which I had brought from England and with the teapot belonging to the negro who makes the beds had my own tea at every station where we fed. We supped at Green River where I made tea for three Englishmen who were in the train and who spent the whole day playing whist. I know nothing about teamaking or tea but have now become, travelling in America, a teetotaller of the most severe kind. We were in snow all day. I am obliged to save time to go back exactly the same way as that by which I came, so I have nothing new to describe.

Friday Oct 17. Very cold. In the train.

We breakfasted at 7 at Rawlings, where there were eight inches of snow. The breakfast was an extremely crude affair as it is not an ordinary halting place. We dined at Laramie and supped at Cheyenne. Here the three Englishmen branched off to Denver, and here for the first time I met with surliness and an unwillingness to supply my teapot with hot water. However I insisted: and got it. But alas! Of all places in the world this was the one which I'd elected to leave my packet of tea in: and so much against my will I rewarded the incivility of the waiters.

Saturday Oct 18. Cold.

It was dark when we reached Omaha, and in the dark we had to change trains, cross the river Missouri and then change trains again. Here I made acquaintance with two sisters travelling alone from San José to Boston. The youngest though she looked 30 was only 16 and the elder not more than 18. There was also a nephew of Musurus Bey who was going on a visit to his uncle in Europe.

It is wonderful this travelling alone of young women in America. They do it with perfect cheerfulness and security, and everywhere gentlemen gladly help them in every way they can, in getting their tickets, or having their luggage checked.

Sunday Oct 19. Finer and milder.

The train went a great pace during the night more than forty miles an hour: a rate of speed which though not absolutely alarming to an Englishman was yet enough for the engine and first car to take the opportunity of running off the track. Happily no one was injured: I was not even awoken.

We arrived at Chicago about three oclock, and I soon drove off to the Grand Pacific Hotel—an enormous building capable of holding 1100 persons. The marble hall was crowded with people, and I soon found Geiger for we had arranged by previous appointment to meet here today. We walked up and down State Street, Wabash Avenue and Michigan Avenue, which, with Clark Street are the principal thoroughfares here.

At 5.30 was dinner and we walked up to a magnificent hall, were handed an apparently endless bill of fare from which we had an excellent dinner without paying or even giving our numbers. On the American system you simply pay four or five dollars a day in which everything is included whether you have it or not. This greatly simplifies their business, but the number of people in this hotel is so great that one cannot help fancying that anyone might walk into the dining room, have dinner and return to the street, without anybody being the wiser.

Geiger and I walked for two or three hours after dinner, and then went to our rooms (which adjoin) on the fourth floor by lift which reminded me of the Grand Hotel in Paris. I had a bath and went to bed.

Monday Oct 20.

GRAND PACIFIC HOTEL, Chicago—very bright and tolerably warm.

We first went today to secure our places in the Pullman car by calling on the secretary of the Pullman Company.

Then to the Exhibition a pretty bright building, happily very small for our ideas of exhibitions. There seemed nothing very startling here except some lovely live birds in cages. There were also a number of tiny bells for the watchchain made out of the metal of the old Chicago alarm bell, so many I may say that as I bought one I could not help congratulating the shopwoman on the enormous size of the original bell; whereat she sniggered.

Afterwards we went to call on General Sheridan—whose headquarters are in Chicago—a short thick set resolute-looking man. There were also Colonel Sheridan his brother and the two Generals ——: both pleasant looking handsome men. Sheridan talked much about hunting but nothing new.

After luncheon we were taken by Colonel Dickie or Dicker a Californian turfite out to Dexter Park to see Goldsmith Maid the most famous trotter America has ever had. She is seventeen years old and trotted her shortest time last week. She is if possible to beat that the day after tomorrow, but she is exceedingly cunning from having run so many hundred races and requires a really good horse and a real not a sham struggle to stimulate her.

After this I got off to the station, and, saying goodbye to Geiger started by the 5.15 train for Niagara. Geiger goes westward.

I had dinner in the hotel car which is pleasant because original; and a long talk with the conductor who was charming as usual.

It may be as well to say here how impossible it is to believe that it is just two years since Chicago was burnt to the ground. The noble streets and the stately buildings show a magnificence and a stability which one cannot well associate with extreme novelty, still less with hurried building. At the same time it must be remembered that this though wonderful itself is a marvellous fact which once realised does not leave very much for the tourist to see in Chicago. I would gladly have seen the great stockyards where are myriads of cattle and pigs are slaughtered by the thousand, gladly have heard Mrs Beecher Stowe give the reading which was announced for this evening, gladly have watched Goldsmith Maid trot the day after tomorrow. But the last two are abnormal sights; the first is the only regular wonder of Chicago.

Tuesday Oct 21. Cold and grey in the train from Chicago to Niagara.

This was a wretched dreary morning. However we arrived at Niagara falls after endless delays at the Suspension bridge about 3, and I put up at the Cataract House. After the 3 oclock dinner which was very hasty I went out to see the falls. I am thankful to say it is unnecessary to describe them.

The place is quite deserted which gives a melancholy and forlorn impression: the day was eminently dreary and cold and colourless. Yet I am not sure that one did not gain by these two apparent disadvantages. By the first one secured solitude and Niagara is one of the things which should be faced alone, and I think the great frenzy of waters gained in wildness and terror by the second.

When one has looked at the waters for a certain time one feels that the mass is alive, that it is a multitude struggling against the resistless current of fate. From the end of the sister islands I gazed on a great waste of waters—turning my back to the fall—a great waste of waters spitting and snarling and flecked with foam like a squally sea—rebelling and protesting against an imperious force they could not resist. And as they neared the chasm and saw their appalling fate and the precipice to which they were hurrying they actually seemed horror stricken to recoil and to make frantic efforts to reascent the cruel flood. And then they were beaten and whirled into space.

Below again there was a broad calm flood oozing slowly away from the great catastrophe sad and serene and hopeless as if the bitterness of Death were past. It seemed as though it were stunned by the crash and were moving on half idle and half unconscious, partly stupefied and partly reckless wherever fate should now order, indifferent where that might be.

At the fall itself the mass is not water but solid and opaque. It is a great thunderbolt being bent over a rampart of rocks.

It is as if when God separated Chaos and bid the earth be severed from the waters, that this great flood was the first joyful bound with which the waves sprang aloof from the uncongenial ground.

And that this alone was allowed to remain as a perpetual monument of the great convulsion of creation, while division became subdivision and subdivision was redivided again, till the primeval fount of fluid ceased to recognize itself in troutstreams.

Wednesday Oct 22. A fine day.
CATARACT HOUSE, Niagara.

Today I drove down to the Whirlpool Rapids. The great rains have made them very full and they are magnificent. But the wily American makes them turn a wheel, and the wheel turns a lift by which one can descend or ascend the rocks.

The whirlpool rapids are a tumult of rage and agony, a hell of waters. When the broad calm stream from the falls finds itself again hurried into a narrow space between mountainous cliffs, whither beyond it knows not, it chafes and storms till the middle of the current stands up in a great ridge feet above the level of the rest of the river. Sometimes one sees a wave that can endure no longer and would return shuddering—but it meets its furious comrades determined that not one shall escape the general curse, there is one great shock, the billows rise into a mountain and the waverer is seen no more. And so on with blind anger ignorant or heedless of their goal but goaded and desperate from the torture they have undergone they thunder on to the serene bank beyond with its pictured bosom bright with melodious colouring and tricked with radiant tints, whence there seems no further outlet to the cruel world, but which promises with all the opulence of autumn a paradise for the weary wanderer and a haven for the betrayed and troubled flood.

At the whirlpool itself which forms this harbour of refuge, and for seeing which and each successive view fifty cents is charged with delightful uniformity (one may truly say "Travellers from the summit of those cliffs for fifty cents are watching you")—there is a great placid pool from which the stream makes a turn at right angles.

I left the Cataract House and Niagara falls at 1 oclock and in company with the Alfred Churchills, a medical student and a gentleman raging with delirium tremens proceeded towards Hamilton and thence to Toronto. The medical student was exceedingly voluble and delighted with the patient but irritated by the refusal of the conductor to allow him to commence a course of treatment on the subject which I gathered from him would end either in a sudden recovery or instant death. Failing this the student discoursed to me of his own medical acquirements. He said he would back himself against most surgeons for removing a leg. He then went off into a general discourse on the amputation of legs which I did not mind, but, what I did mind, never taking his eyes off my leg: he also mentioned that he had all the instruments ready at hand, and this in so marked a manner that I had at last to beg that he would dismiss all designs on my leg for I was foolishly attached to it: which remark he received with compassionate good humour.

At Hamilton we parted from him which he professed to regret very much, but I think he secretly felt that he could carry out his designs on our delirious friend more successfully alone.

From Hamilton to Toronto the journey is about two hours, which I spent principally outside the cars. At Toronto the Churchills halted.

At Toronto there was a frenzied rush for sleeping places—not one was to be had. Honourable members and members reputed by the Pacific railroad enquiry somewhat dishonourable struggle in vain. I at last got a berth over a gentleman (and a pleasant gentleman) the secretary of the evangelical alliance respecting which he said he would send me 'a few papers'. He said the reception of the Alliance in America had been princely, and instanced their being sent from New York to Washington in a special train that cost the railway company which 'treated' them four thousand dollars.

I afterwards got another lower berth (the lower berths are the best) but had to change at Prescott Junction for Ottawa at about six or seven oclock in the morning. From Prescott to Ottawa I was in the same carriage with Sir Hugh Allan, the leading notoriety of the scandal.

Thursday Oct 23.

RUSSELL HOUSE, Ottawa—raw and cold.

I arrived at Ottawa about ten. I had a room at the Russell House, having long preengaged it, but fifty or sixty people were sent empty away. I found a note from Dufferin insisting on my coming out to Rideau House, but I decided for various reasons that I would not go there till Saturday. However on first reading the note I told the clerk that I should very likely have to give up my room soon. On which a gentleman with a red beard began hectoring and bullying the clerk and insisting on having my room. "At last" I said to myself "I have found the insolent and domineering American so well known to the readers of English books on America". Alas! it was the English aide de camp, Mr Clayden, of Joseph Arch who stood by. I was sorry to discover this, on various grounds, which it is needless now to enter upon, and I was perhaps unduly disappointed in Joseph Arch's face. Weary at last of hearing the aide de camp swaggering over the civil clerk, I respectfully suggested to him that it was not all certain that I should vacate my room. It was whistling to a cyclone; he continued to empty vials on the wretched clerk, who vainly endeavoured to prove to him that the first comers must be first served that he had sixty names waiting in rotation for vacancies but that he would do his best for the two gentlemen. But Clayden continued to insist that their claims were paramount, that they would 'put up with' my room (which happened to be the best in the hotel) till they could be suitably accommodated.

I have dwelt, perhaps unduly, on this scene to give myself a wholesome lesson against hasty judgements. Englishmen would at once have rushed to the conclusion that this man was a 'Yankee' or a low Englishman. As it happened he was an Englishman and of a class much superior to Joseph Arch who stood quietly by like a true gentleman.

As soon as I was dressed I went out to Rideau House where I found Dufferin and Lady Dufferin dressed and diamonded for the coming ceremony, and G. Brodrick and Rutson, and the two aides de camp Ward and Hamilton, and Tarbat and Mr Rothery the Fisheries commissioner under the treaty of Washington.

I was in the House long before they arrived (in evening dress) and met R. Russell and Dallas Mr Rothery's two aides, who introduced me to the Speaker of the Senate and the Usher of the Black Rod. The latter got me a good seat on the cross benches as it were of the House. On each side of the throne were places for the Speaker of the Senate and Lady Dufferin who faced each other. Dufferin was rather late having to open a new road and bridge, but arrived at last and sat on the throne very fine in an uniform and cocked hat.

The faithful commons were summoned with their mace to the bar and the speech was read by Dufferin first in English and then in French. On Dufferin's right there stood a clerk holding the mace of the Senate, ladies sat all round (the prettiest of them was Miss Lewis the bishop's daughter), and the front seats one deep were occupied by some shaky old gentlemen in evening dress and large ill fitting gloves who represented the Senate—the feudal aristocracy of Canada. The institution is I understand a farce and has all the appearance of it.

Dufferin had to read his speech first in English and then in French: taking off his hat whenever he addressed the House by its titles.

After this we went to the Commons where some formal business was transacted and Sir John moved an adjournment till Monday in order to give members time to read the report of the Commission.

This evening Patteson the editor of the 'Mail' the Toronto Conservative organ gave Senator Macpherson and myself dinner at the Rideau Club: a small club-house opposite the parliament buildings.

Friday Oct 24.

RUSSELL HOUSE—a lovely day.

Today I walked with R. Russell (who is here with Rothery the commissioner on Fisheries) to the end of the main street where there is a pretty view of Ottawa and the Chaudière falls. It is a very pleasant looking city with immense piles of clean looking and clean smelling timber and the wild woods reaching down into the town. After luncheon a large party of us including Mr Mitchell minister of Marine and Patteson the Conservative Editor set out under the guidance of Messrs Wright (a very paunchy man) Batson (a rather wild pleasant looking fellow) and Currier (member for Ottawa) to see the leviathan saw mills belonging to these last. Mr Currier I believe took his wife there on her wedding day; she caught in a machine and was cut to pieces before his eyes.

The mills are magnificent, and it is curious to see the whole process by which the rugged old forest patriarch finds himself snapped up from the river before he knows what he is after and is sawn straight and smooth into monotony.

There is a slide down to the river in which the great trunks are floating. Down this slide is hurried a carriage with grappling hooks. The carriage goes right under water—a man guides two logs over it—the carriage is pulled up and it is found that the grappling hooks have safely gaffed the timber. Thence it is passed up against a huge saw that divides it into planks.

After inspecting the works, we adjourned to a neighbouring room where several bottles of champagne were produced, before which we sat for an hour and a half. This is an inevitable but alarming form of Canadian hospitality.

Afterwards we drove to the great lucifer match factory where there is a most beautiful machine for cutting wood into matches which was so perfect that one could watch it for any amount of time. Then the quickness with which the girls (all French) put the matches into the boxes was marvellous. Everything seemed to be on fire but the wood being wet, no one seemed to care.

Thence we went to the Chaudière falls, which are perfect in

their way, and can be seen in a much more complete compass of course than Niagara, while at the same time they assist one to realise it. For here one sees the prodigious force of the volume of water, which of course is fifty times greater at Niagara. Here too there is a deep pool surrounded by cataracts, which is peculiar to it and gives a remarkably fine effect. Moreover as we saw it in the serenity of a glorious sunset which stilled the waters to glass with one hand and darkened the great woods with the other, the Chaudière 'quadilateral' of cascades had a very noble appearance.

Patteson gave a dinner this evening to us: and he had Sir F. Hincks, Senator Macpherson, Mr Plumb of Niagara and Mr Rutson exsecretary to Bruce in the Home Office. I innocently set Hincks and Macpherson by the ears after dinner on the scandal they being opposing interests of the most pronounced kind. Plumb is a very pleasant genial and gentlemanlike person, a naturalised American, with a considerable sense of humour.

He walked with me up and down the street for half an hour telling me about Arch's views as expressed to him at his own house the other day.

Saturday Oct 25.
WALKER HOUSE. Ottawa—fine but cold.

This morning I breakfasted with Huntington at the Club. Mr Edgar the opposition whip a gentlemanlike man was there: and after breakfast he shewed me over the House of Commons, the library and the lovers' walk which is right round the height on which the building is situated. He introduced me to Mr Alpheus Todd the librarian, Mr Mackenzie the leader of the Opposition and Mr Blake its champion.

All the buildings are extremely handsome and convenient. The House of Commons was crowded, because it is used as a club, each man writing letters or reading newspapers at his own desk.

After this I packed up and paid my bill (22 dollars for two nights) at the Russell House. What has really most impressed me here is

IV. THE DANCE-HALL AT THE "WICKEDEST MAN'S" HOUSE

V.   MIDSUMMER IN THE FIVE POINTS

being made to pay 25 cents or 1s. $\frac{1}{2}d$. for each time by boots are blacked.

I then set out for Rideau Hall. After luncheon we looked on at some athletic sports for a short time and then I walked into Ottawa with Macpherson and Plumb to dine with Huntington. When I arrived however I found the preparations on such a noble scale that I hurried back in a carriage to dress.

It was a large party. Huntington at first proposed to put me in a room alone and bring in the company to be introduced. This I declined as a greater evil than being led round, as I was, and introduced to everybody in turn. I sat between Huntington and Edgar and opposite Blake. There were moreover Mr Holton (a leading member of the opposition) Mr Appleby, Mr Laflamme, Mr Cutler, Mr Paquet, Dr St Georges, Mr Pelter, (these two very pleasant Frenchmen) Mr Mackay of Cape Breton, Mr Thomson, Mr Coffin, M. Cauchon (member for Quebec) and many others whose names I cannot remember except a Mr Burpee.

There was some subdued excitement about Mackay. He is a young supporter of the government who is going to vote for the opposition. Lady Macdonald has sent for him in the afternoon to make a personal appeal to him, and as he did not arrive till an hour after we sat down, there were fears that that appeal had been successful. However he did at last turn up and was reputed staunch. Huntington proposed my health in a speech, I took care to reply only in a word, as the capital is in such a state of excitement and party feeling is so high that it was better to say nothing on any subject. I remained till 12 when St Georges and Peltier walked home with me to Rideau. St Georges can hardly speak English.

Sunday Oct 26.

RIDEAU HALL (Govt. House). Ottawa—rainy.

I did not go to church, nor did I go out all day. Nor indeed have I anything personal to record today, which is

3

a good thing, as, to be frank, I am behind hand with this valuable record.

Monday Oct 27.

Today was the beginning of the great debate. I got a chair on the floor of the house next to the speaker. The house met at 3. The address was moved by Mr Witton (a working man) who spoke for about ¾ of an hour dealing with every paragraph. The seconder M. Baby member for Joliette (it sounds like an opera of Offenbach's) whose name is pronounced like the bawbee of my beloved country only spoke for twenty minutes and in French. Then came Mr Mackenzie leader of Her Majesty's Canadian opposition. He is an obstinate-looking, long-upper-lipped Scotchman, with the peculiarly aggravating unintelligent manner of an intelligent middle aged Scotsman. He is a great credit to Scotland, having been a working mason, 15 or 20 years ago. He is, it appears, hardheaded, dry, sarcastic, and universally respected.

Then came an adjournment at 6 for dinner—which lasted till 7.45. Brodrick and I dined with Senator Macpherson in one of the dining rooms of the Senate. The company besides ourselves were Senator Christie an Edinburgh man, keen farmer and opposition Senator, Mr Kirkpatrick a young government member, Mr Thomson a Scotsman, with an extraordinary financial theory much dreaded by his friends, Rutson and Plumb. After dinner we returned to the house where Dr. Tupper a cabinet minister and accoucheur spoke on a variety of topics for three hours. He was followed by Huntington in a speech of two hours which required more preparation than it had received and which finished with several pages of Macaulay's 'History' treating of the duke of Leeds' disgrace. Although read out with considerable unction it failed to impress the audience, who were apparently quite bewildered as to what it all referred to. Huntington has a charming voice a good delivery and great quickness, but I suspect he does not take much preliminary trouble with his speeches.

Tuesday Oct 28.

RIDEAU HALL, Ottawa—rainy.

I went into Ottawa in the morning with Tarbat but was not particularly successful in doing what I wanted. Lunched at Rideau,
but at three was on the floor of the house, ready for everything.
Our first speaker was Sir Francis Hincks who is mixed up in the
affair. All the chivalry of Canada is I am sorry to say implicated—
Sir Hugh Allan, Sir John Macdonald, Sir George Cartier, Sir F.
Hincks—there is not a stainless knight in Canada: unless the
scandal be altogether unfounded. As however, Sir Hugh Allan has
already been dubbed by New York papers "the champion liar of
the American continent", a sort of halo of championship still
clings to him.

After Sir Francis' vehement speech of an hour Huntington rose
and contradicted an allegation of Sir Francis' that he (Huntington)
had spread and originated a report of Sir John Macdonald's having
committed suicide. Then came Macdonald of Pictou—not a
feudal chieftain, but always called after his constituency to distinguish him from others of the same name. He spoke better than
anybody we had yet heard and for two hours and a half.

In the middle of his speech I dined with Patteson as the adjournment for dinner came then.

After Macdonald came Glass a recreant supporter of Government who with stately periods excused his conduct. These however
were much interfered with by a gentleman who represented the
appropriate constituency of Niagara, and kept dashing into
Glass's speech from an adjoining desk with insulting remarks. "If
the member of Niagara" at last exclaimed the unhappy Glass "has
any public accusation to bring against me let him rise in his place".
Unluckily however Niagara preferred vilifying him from a chair,
and Niagara finally overwhelmed Glass. Glass was succeeded by
an orator much in his own style who attempted to crush Glass by
sonorous sentences but was unable to effect much, though I thought
his manner promised well. However it turned out afterwards that
he had been ordered to speak unexpectedly. His name is Baker and

his constituency is Missisquoi. He was followed by one of those remarkable orators who never fail to fill me with dumb admiration. With a skill almost miraculous he plodded steadily over the beaten track without once for an instant getting out of the footsteps of his predecessors or uttering an idea which had not received the sanction of all of them. He could only be compared to an intellectual egg-dancer, skipping lightly about without even grazing the shell of a thought. This heroic member Mr Young represented Waterloo. I was the only stranger who sat out his hour and a quarter. When the house rose it was half past eleven, pitch dark and a snowstorm. So these advantages I added an imperfect knowledge of my way home and a large bundle of newspapers lent me by Patteson. I never had such a walk—the mud was up to my shins—I could not see where I was walking and the snow and sleet came down with a will. The distance is not a mile and a half but it took me more than an hour. However it had an end like most things. I thought I should have had one too from a large black watchdog. Luckily he did nothing but growl.

Wednesday Oct 29—deep snow.

Tarbat and I were photographed this morning, having offered while looking at photographs to be taken if the man could manage it at once. The result was a photograph of me looking like a ghoul with Tarbat in a sort of tipsy attitude in front. This portrait was soon known as the 'demon and the drunkard'.

The sitting today at the whole of which I assisted as usual from three till 11.30 exclusive of the dinner interval was taken up by two speakers. The next day I was asked by a Canadian gentleman what I thought of the speeches. I replied that they were longer than English speeches, that speeches of four or five hours were almost unknown in England. "Ah, but" said my friend compassionately "in England you have no speakers whom you could listen to for four or five hours". I mildly suggested that I thought we had that Mr Gladstone—"No" he interrupted me firmly but kindly "No, there are none such now. Possibly the late Earl of Derby—but none now". What was I to say?

The first orators were Mr Wood member for South Dinham who spoke for five hours. In the course of his speech he denounced the oratorical and obstetrical Tupper as 'a Lucifer, a fallen star'. "He will rise again" shouted Sir John Macdonald. "Not till the last trump" retorted Wood with energy, and the opposition cheered with enthusiasm, and indeed well they might.

We dined with Rothery at the Russell House. There was a lottery on the division which I would not join.

The second orator was Palmer the member for Saint John's, who had good cause to be angry for had he not been told by Mr Glass that his foot was physically as well as morally large? The second portion of which taunt remains after much careful study a complete mystery to me. Moreover Mr Glass had held him up to ridicule as having been bathing his ample form in the Bay of Fundy when he ought to have been in parliament. These sarcasms, though parliamentary were unendurable, and Palmer struck boldly into the debate,—to keep up the Fundy metaphor (observe I keep clear of puns such as 'fundamental' etc.). However he was much interrupted, and indeed his speech (as I have already compared one to an egg dance I will keep to my figure) was as if Sir Roger Tichborne should try and perform an entrechat in fishing boots. He was so much harassed that he threatened at the next interruption to adjourn. Human nature could not resist such a temptation, and he was at once interrupted: so we adjourned. The only notable event afterwards was that my cabdriver attempted to charge me four dollars and a half (18s. 9d.) for driving me (a mile and a half at the most) to Rideau Hall. The worm will turn and I resisted.

Thursday Oct 30—bright and cold.

I remained in all this morning, and except for walking under the veranda with Brodrick all the afternoon. I dined at Rideau and afterwards went to the House. Kirkpatrick, a pleasant young

Irish lawyer but a doubtful Grattan, was finishing his defence of the government. Then came Mr Macdonald member for Glengarry who announced that he had a cold in his head (which was quite unnecessary). This soon brought him to an end. Then came Dr Grant who had attended Sir John in an illness lately and had then recognised in him those powers which had made him famous throughout the civilised world. After describing Sir John's symptoms and sentiments he declared his belief that Providence had produced Sir John with an eye to the Pacific railway.

Then came Mr Cunningham of Manitoba who praised Sir John and denounced the government. He was a racy speaker and it appearing to him that it was a good opportunity now that he was on his legs to work off anything on his mind, he gave his views as to the laxity of the government in keeping its promises to Manitoba, and dealt at length with the question of Louis Riel.

Then followed Thomson of Cariboo who defended the government as usual by attacking the opposition. Him succeeded M. Joly, a very gentlemanlike French Canadian who had arrived from England in the midst of the debate and produced I think a great impression by repeating the terms of censure which were there universally used towards the behaviour of this government.

Then came Wallace member for Norfolk an elderly man. This was his second speech, his first having failed through nervousness which he has now at any rate completely overcome. His peroration was notable—"we are sent here to maintain the majesty of parliament, and, and and and" (great difficulty and wild search for a tag) "the dignity and honour of God".

The House then adjourned, and Wallace's friends gave him a hip hip hurrah.

Friday Oct 31, Ottawa—dull.

Went in to Ottawa with Hamilton and Tarbat. We were out again for luncheon, but in again for the debate at three. This was opened by Tilley of New Brunswick, minister of finance, who spoke very well and to the point. But his ending, considering that he was a minister, was sufficiently amusing: that having in view who the ministry were and who their successors would be, he should, on that account alone, vote 'Not Guilty'.

He was followed by Mr Laflamme of the opposition, a very gentlemanlike French Canadian who however spoke in English. I could not well catch what he said.

As this was my last night at Rideau I dined there and did not return to the House: more especially as no good speakers were expected or indeed possible.

Saturday Nov 1.

RIDEAU HALL, Ottawa—fine but cold.

I walked in with Fletcher to see if Sir John was going to speak on Monday, which might have detained me. But he wrote to say there was but little chance of this, so after luncheon, I started for Quebec, viâ Prescott and Montreal. One leaves at 2 p.m. and gets in at 8 a.m.

Great part of the way (from Prescott to Montreal) I travelled with the president of the Senate M. Chauveau, his daughter, her friend a girl, and the Editor of the Minerve. The last two carried on a desperate flirtation, which, as being under his immediate wing shocked the president, I think.

Sunday Nov 2.

ST LOUIS HOTEL, Quebec—fine in morning but very cold.

At Point Levi opposite Quebec one leaves the train and is ferried across the St Lawrence. Here my luggage was left in spite of the solemn assurances of the railway officials who said it was checked to Quebec. Here it remained all the Sabbath as no other boat crosses the river on Sunday. This is holy but inconvenient.

The views round Quebec in the early morning were divine. Its situation is much as if a town had been built over the Castle rock at Edinburgh, only that it is surrounded by a river. The streets are narrow quaint and winding. I drove out in the afternoon to see the Plains of Abraham on which are now situated the local prison and a monument to Wolfe. The monument is a column erected in 1849 to replace the one of 1832 put up by General Lord Aylmer and the English army and which had been defaced. The 1832 column is now buried under the 1849 column which was also the gift of the English troops in Canada, and which bears an explanatory inscription besides these few words "Here Wolfe died victorious" or "Here died Wolfe victorious Sept 13 1759".

Thence I drove out to the Montmorenci falls 7 miles from the city. The bridge toll is remarkable. I payed 11 cents ($5\frac{1}{2}d.$) going out. Coming back I hoped to get through for nothing: no, 12 cents. "Why 12 ? I only paid 11 before". "That will make 23", was the only explanation I got. This shews how unsatisfactory the strictest truth may be.

On my way I saw the lunatic asylum and a pretty villa with greenhouses (great rarities) belonging to Dr Douglas who had been the asylum doctor. Then there was an old French house which had been Montcalm's head quarters, and a column erected to Temperance by Father Mathew. The Montmorenci falls are very wild. The adjoining cliffs are more rugged and savage than anything at Niagara, and the cataract not being so broad *seems* higher. It commands a beautiful view of Quebec. A crowd of little French boys came with me. "I show the falls to mis-ter" was their perpetual cry. If I explained to them that I meant to see the falls alone, they all began again as if each was soliloquizing "I show the falls to mis-ter". This failing, they began to address me "you give me a cop-per-mis-ter-". At last they left me, but I have seen nothing like them out of Italy.

It was bitterly cold—a cutting wind and icy rain.

Monday Nov 3.

ST LOUIS HALL, Quebec—rainy morning, fine afternoon.

While I was breakfast[ing] the Mayor called on me. Dufferin had telegraphed to him to ask him to do so. He is a most charming Frenchman (★His name is Garneau, I think). He had known my uncle (like almost everyone) and took me to see his house—a handsome yellow house with a 'Grecian' front and a glorious view over the bay. Then we went to the Citadel, where Major Montizambert a very pleasant artillery officer shewed us over the fortress, from which there are magnificent views. It is place of immense strength built over and round the old French battlements which are still seen, crumbling. It has three subsidiary forts on the Point Levi side of the river, which the British erected just before they withdrew their troops. All these forts are in good order.

In the artillery museum I saw a 'parachute light'. It is a balloon enclosed in a shell. The shell bursts and the parachute emerges over the heads of the enemy burning a light to show what they are doing.

After leaving the citadel we saw St John and St Roch's Catholic churches—both of them enormous—with pews which pay high rents but which I never saw in a Catholic church before. Then to the Custom House, built like much of the Low town, on encroachment from the Sea. Then to the parliament house. Then through the principal streets to the Stadacona Club where I was introduced and eat a dozen of Cacarette (or some such name) oysters. I liked Quebec immensely but have no time to dwell on it properly.

After dinner I left for Montreal where I arrived about 7 am.

November 4.

ST LAWRENCE HALL, Montreal—fine but cold.

After walking about the streets—there are two principal ones Nôtre Dame and Great St James Street in which latter is my hotel.

3*

I went and bought a walking stick spiked for winter, and a buffalo robe at Maciver's. Then to the meet of the Montreal foxhounds. It was an iron frost, 'but they like that all the better' I was told. However only two liked it besides the whips (the field being sometimes fifteen or twenty) and I soon came back. I was hunting like Queen Anne in a one horse conveyance.

After luncheon I went up to the top of the Cathedral tower and saw a magnificent view of Montreal, which does not however appear as busy and increasing as I expected. Thence to see the shipping and the Bonsecours market—a magnificent building; and to walk all over the town. After dinner I went to hear 'Gerald Massey the great English lecturer and Poet' (*his real name Mercy of the Mentmore[1] family) discourse on the 'Sea-Kings of England'.

He is a small man (though Heaven forbid I should speak ill of small men) with a mean presence, a shrill voice, a rank growth of hair, and a very decent love of buncombe and bloodshed. As he stood behind a table extending his hands in a fine frenzy he was exactly like a linendraper's young man measuring a length of calico behind a counter. For an hour and a half the Poet discoursed to us in a flowing style about 'the blue boundlessness of the sea', the Hebrew origin of Ashridge where he lives, the 'old Norse spirit' which 'made Disraeli fight for the Corn Laws', (heavens, how this would astonish Dizzy!) and 'the great heart of England beating responsive in ours'. It was sublime, and my feelings overcame me so in the first five minutes that I would have given worlds to give vent to my emotions outside. But I was in an inner place and could not move. And now the worst remains. Let no one read the coming passage. I occupied room No 129 in the hotel, divided from 130 by a thin door. The poet occupied No 130. In the middle of the night I was awoke by a thunder as of artillery. What event had happened? Was it a revolution? Was the Queen going to marry again? Were Beale and Inman bankrupt? Alas! a moment's reflection shewed the truth—I can hardly tell it—the Poet snored like a trooper.

1. The home of Rosebery's future wife, Hannah de Rothschild.

Wednesday Nov 5.
ST LAWRENCE HALL, Montreal—a lovely day.

This morning by the 8.40 train I left Montreal for Boston where I arrived at 10.45 p.m. This was a very well run journey, the train was empty and before its time at every station. The scenery in Vermont from St Albans to White River Junction was really beautiful, much aided by the delicate lights.

My conductor was a pleasant fellow. He had been a hotel keeper for sixteen years—for the five last at Montreal—up to last year. I did not ask him how he fell. His experience as a hotel keeper had made him hate negroes.

I put up at the Revere House, where I found a letter from my mother, the first I have received from England.

Thursday Nov 6—a fine day.
REVERE HOUSE, Boston.

Here I am capitally situated in the Revere House on the ground floor in No 4 room. And Boston blest among cities! Here it is that for the first time I have got my journal square. After breakfast Mr Ignatius Sargent, a nephew of Mrs Duncan's to whom she had written, came and took me to the Somerset club where he introduced me and shewed me over. From 12 till 2.45 I wrote Journal (which now I will with feelings of infinite relief abandon for the day) and was shaved and wrote a long letter to Hurlbert and did a variety of indoor things.

I then called upon Prescott the son of the historian with whom I had crossed in the 'Russia'. He was suffering from his eyes, but introduced me to his wife and daughter Edith.

I also left a letter and card on Mr Winthrop. I dined at the hotel, and after dinner strolled into an old bookseller's. We fell into conversation. He is an enthusiastic Scot named Campbell. He was born in the north of Ireland and has never been in Scotland. I told him I was Scotch, upon which he observed "Eh, I knew it from your accent as you came in"! This remark I shall spread as a testimonial in Scotland.

Campbell, full of ardour, always (from three years ago) is bringing over Scotch books. Though he has only been at it three years he receives orders for Scotch books from 1000 miles off. He printed a catalogue of his Scotch books. He had in it one copy of Buchanan's Latin history of Scotland. He despaired of selling this but soon got *two* orders for it. He is quite an enthusiast and quite a character, bringing out the most ordinary Scotch works and thrusting them at me with an air of defiance "Well, anyhow, you never saw the like of that". All this ardent Scotch feeling is united with a shrewd American face and accent.

Friday Nov 7—fine.
REVERE HOUSE, Boston.

This morning Mr Joseph Peabody Gardner to whom I had a letter called to take me a drive round about Boston. However Mr Winthrop (Robert C. Winthrop) called too and took us both off to the Massachusetts Historical Society, of which he is president. There I saw Benjamin Franklin's coat which he wore when Wedderburn denounced to him and laid by to wear at the signing of the treaty of Paris: a faded plum coloured garment. There are many other curiosities, curious old portraits, one the only existing contemporary portrait of a Pilgrim father: the swords of Colonel Prescott and Captain Linsee who fought against each other at the Battle of Bunker Hill, but whose families and swords became united by the marriage of Prescott the historian with a descendant of Captain Linsee's. Prescott always kept these swords hung up in his library (where Thackeray who alludes to them in the 'Virginians', saw them) and bequeathed them to the Historical Society. Here also is the sword of Miles Standish.

Then we went to the Public Library, where all who run in

Boston may read, greatly aided by the munificence of Mr Bates, the father of Madame Van de Weyer. Here is a picture of Copley's "Charles the First demanding the arrest of the Five Members", in which, though the colouring and grouping is good, the king is made to appear not a man of conviction engaging in a struggle of life and death or even a monarch demanding what he conceives to be a right, but a mere careless coxcomb the prey of a whim.

After this Mr Gardner drove me all round about the city and its environs Charleston, Chelsea and so. He took me so carefully through the scene of the fire and entered into so circumstantial a description of it that I got quite dazed and began to fancy myself a sort of dreamy insurance office. (O damned and damnable pen!)

We took luncheon at the Somerset club. Afterwards I went with Mr. Winthrop to see the Charity Bureau, a sort of charity organization society in a building erected by the city for the purpose and which also contains the municipal officers of outdoor relief. (The system here is municipal not parochial.) I spent the rest of the afternoon in Piper's, a bookshop.

I dined with Mr and Mrs Prescott at 84 Beacon Street. There were also dining Dr and Mrs Warren (she a Miss Amy Shaw a noted Boston beauty) and Mr Lawrence junior a good looking or pleasant looking student at Cambridge (this one here) and a grandson of a Mr Lawrence who was minister at our court. Prescott's eyes were too bad for him to dine, but otherwise we had a very pleasant dinner.

Saturday Nov 8.

REVERE HOUSE, Boston—rainy morning, fine afternoon.

This morning I saw as much of the public schools as possible, which was not much as they close at 12 on Saturdays. I went with Dr Lothrop chairman of the 'English High School' and of the City School Board (which has 96 members or so), and Mr Philbrick the superintendent of public schools. We went over a primary school for boys and girls, a grammar school for boys and girls, and the English High School which Bishop Fraser praises so highly in his report. Everything appeared perfection, the ventilation, the single desks, the bright looks, the gentle method of teaching and its (to us) enormous practical range. Moreover, the social equality is said to be complete, though the rich boy gives his cast off clothes to the master for his poorer classmate. The head boy in the grammar school was a Japanese who by wonderful industry, quickness and singleness of application had overtaken the other boys. In the girl's grammar school there was a brightlooking coloured girl, who was said to do very well. In the high school the quickest pupils apparently were a number of Jew boys (who on Saturday attend but will not put pen to paper) who solved intricate mentals sums of interest with startling rapidity. From the schools, of which here it is impossible to give a full account so that it is better to give none at all, we went to the drill hall, where, twice a week, the schools are drilled with carbines. This again was exceedingly interesting, and the moral effect of the responsibility of the boy officers was said to be excellent in the schools outside the drillhall. After this I went off alone to Cambridge to find Mr Cary but unluckily missed him, though I saw—vidi tantum—professor Agassiz, a broad man with a genial powerful face, who was pointed out to me passing us.

I spent my afternoon in bookstalls after this, Piper's where I laid out 91 dollars, and Campbell's, where I visited more as a friend and was introduced to the old man's son. He is full of going to Scotland and of corresponding with Stillie.

Then I set off to dine with Mr and Mrs Winthrop. There were present their daughter Miss Winthrop and their niece Miss ——, Mr Brooks the great preacher here, Dr Holmes 'the autocrat of the Breakfast table', and Mr Emery the father in law of my cicerone Mr Gardner.

Dr Holmes is a little man with a bright mobile face an almost feminine softness of manner, and a certain sort of indescribable halo of bookishness and unworldliness. He was extremely pleasant. After dinner Mr and Mrs Perkins came in. I walked home with Mr Emery.

Sunday Nov 9. Boston—mild and fine.

Today I met Mr Winthrop who took me to St Paul's church where Mr Brooks was to preach. The church was a hideous 'Grecian' temple of the earlier part of the century made a perfect hell by recent painting in the Pompeian style.

Mr Brooks conducted the service himself. He read rapidly and I should think indistinctly for those any way off. He put on the black Geneva gown before the sermon and said his private prayer by the communion table before mounting the pulpit.

He preached an admirable sermon (though I have heard much better) on Deut. 23. 16.

He dealt entirely with the difference between the young and the mature Christian. His manner is breathlessly quick, and he reads every word so that he has no time for elaborate elocution or oratorical gesture. There were some very eloquent passages notably one where he talked of the holy places in the world, those places where different individuals had first heard the voice of God in their hearts. He appeared by implication to treat all Christianity as a sort of revival which occurs in early manhood or afterwards. He preached fully three quarters of an hour.

The pew belonged to Mr Winthrop's eldest son, to whom with his wife I was introduced. He asked about Dalmeny[1] through which he had driven, and the horse committee in which he appeared to take an interest.

Mr Cary called on me at the hotel, and was very agreeable, telling stories about Sam Ward in their early Californian life. He remained about an hour, and I then crossed the street to Senator Sumner who is lodging at the Coolidge House, with whom I remained two hours and a half.

He was in his dressing gown, and with his large head and flowing grey hair presented a sufficiently impressive appearance. His mouth is a large powerful oratorical mouth, implying I think more the faculty of expressing than character. His eyes are small and too close together. But he is imposing taken as a whole, and very charming as a talker, without or nearly without the American

1. Rosebery's ancestral home in Scotland.

tendency to lecture, and having gentle cadences in his voice and a pleasant smile.

After leaving him I called upon the Prescotts and took leave of them. I then dined at the hotel and spent the rest of the evening in my room.

Today was the anniversary of the Great fire of Boston which is said to have destroyed property worth seventy millions of dollars. It is rather curious that I should have happened to be in Boston and Chicago on their dismal anniversaries.

Nov 10—a lovely day.

This morning I left Boston by the ten oclock train and reached New York at 5.15. The country seemed lovely in the sunlight, at any rate the country from Newhaven to New York.

Sam Ward was patiently pacing the street in front of the hotel waiting for me, and at once hurried me down to a cellar next his own: not a pleasant room but sociable.

I gave Hurlbert and him dinner at the hotel. Afterwards we went to the opera meeting the Duncans on the steps. The piece was the 'Huguenots', and Nilsson disappointed me less than usual, while Campanini sang really well. After this Johnny Balfour and Hurlbert and Ward and I adjourned to an oyster supper at Delmonico's. Did not get to bed till half past two.

Jay Gould was at the opera and pointed out to me. He is a short man, not forty I should think, with a black beard and a bright eye.

Nov 11.

BREVOORT HOUSE, New York—a lovely day.

Sam Ward and I breakfasted together, and afterwards drove out to see the trotting at Fleetwood Park. It was a fine day and wonderfully clear while the road was gay with trotters and sulkies[1] flashing past like minnows in a stream.

The great event of the day was a match between Judge Fullerton and American Girl. The first second and fourth heats were won pretty easily by the horse, but the third was a magnificent race and resulted in a dead heat.

There is a Mr Bonner, the proprietor of a paper called the 'Ledger', who owns a stable of trotters worth 50000 £. They are never allowed to race, but he keeps them for his own driving. For one, 'Dexter', the most famous trotter in America he gave $35000 or £7000. This for a horse to drive in one's private gig is pretty well.

Sam Ward gave dinner to Hurlbert and myself at Sutherland's. After dinner he left for Washington, and Hurlbert and I went to Barnum's circus. I love circuses for the simple reason that they are the reductio ad absurdum of amusements.

There are two arenas in Barnum's great tent so that two performances are going on at once. Of course they were what we know so well, the tittupping piebald, the stale joke and the perforated hoop.

Afterwards Hurlbert took me to his charming rooms and shewed me some of his household goods. He has some pretty paintings, and his furniture and decorations are suggestive, so that his eye rests perpetually on objects which bring his imagination to every place he has ever visited. I was particularly struck with his having a scarlet biretta as a lamp cover—quite a stroke of genius for recalling Rome. I went to bed early.

Nov 12.

BREVOORT HOUSE, New York—cold and rainy.

I wrote in the morning, and lunched with the Duncan's. Went in the afternoon to Tiffany's, *the* smart shop of New York. I asked for American productions, after buying the (English) umbrella

1. Carriages so called because they only took one person.

which was my object, and was shewn some tortoiseshell ornaments and some silver jewelry. This appeared to be all that was purely American in the shop. I suspect working jewellers and labourers in small articles of luxury have not been much attracted to this country as yet, and it is much cheaper even with the high tariffs to import such things from Europe. Even the walking sticks here and in Canada, come, not from the Virgin forests of the New World as one might expect, but from Brigg of St. James' Street and the dealers of the British Isles.

I dined with the Belmonts, that is Mr and Mrs August Belmont and their nice daughter, Mrs Heckster, and Dr —— from the English Embassy at Pekin. Afterwards we moved on to the opera where Nilsson and Campanini sang again in the 'Huguenots'. The great panic has had a disastrous effect, and the manager has been compelled to reduce Nilsson's salary from 1000 to 600 dollars a night. M. Rouzeaud Nilsson's happy husband was there tonight in a box. He appears capable of playing the proper rôle of effacé to admiration: which is a useful power in the husband of a great singer.

Thursday Nov 13.

BREVOORT HOUSE, New York—very cold.

Sam Ward returned from Washington this morning with a political pamphlet, the illustrations to 'Justine', and two brace of Canvasbacks under his arm! This illustrates him wonderfully well.

We breakfasted together: after which Hurlbert came and took me to Bouton's an old book-seller at 706 Broadway. After buying a little we went down town to a place where Hurlbert entertained us at luncheon. There were Mr Harper (head of the publishing firm), Major Constable (Harper's superintendent and son of the great Edinburgh Constable), Mr Sievers editor of Harper's Monthly and Mr Osgood the Boston publisher.

We afterwards went over the great publishing house of Harper's —the greatest in the world. They use I think $7\frac{1}{2}$ tons of paper daily, and their electrotyping process improved by the intelligent head electrotyper is the most perfect known. The size of the place, the army of workmen, the arsenal of books, and the momentary adding to their number by the huge pitiless machines with the enormous implied influence on human thought and therefore on human action, impressed me so much that I had to ask Hurlbert to tie me down in the homeward omnibus for fear I should be didactic. Major Constable is a tall soldierlike and agreeable man. He said he used to go as a child to Dalmeny to play with my father and uncle.

On my return I found Tarbat who had arrived in New York from Ottawa.

I dined with the Duncans to go with them to the opera. Senator Thurman the leader of the Democrats dined there too. It being expected of me that I should talk gravely to him, I need not say I said and committed every absurdity that I could think of. Of such are not the kingdom of Heaven. The opera was at the Lyceum— Lucca and Ilma da Murska in the 'Flauto Majico'. All went well till the second act when the chorus appeared with long horns which they blew, as was proper, and then waited for the High Priest. The High Priest however would not appear. The band now played the overture and music in general. Then the chorus disappeared, trooping off amid the derision of the audience. They then drew up the scene and exposed another on which we feasted our eyes for some time: they then put back the original scene. Then Lucca moved I suppose by sudden impulse came on and sang something but finding no support disappeared. At last Jamet the high priest appeared and sang his solo, but he was sulky and his voice boomed at us in a dreadful manner. All was of a piece, it was a Comedy of Errors.

We all walked home including the ladies, and I gave supper to Hurlbert, Ward and Balfour and Tarbat. It was a very cheery party and the supper did Delmonico credit: while an anecdote of Sam's about seven bottles of absinthe and South America lasted about an hour, the point being ultimately omitted.

Friday. Nov 14.

BREVOORT HOUSE, New York—very cold.

This morning Sam Ward and I started to see the collection of trotting horses belonging to Mr Bonner, the Editor of the 'Weekly Ledger'. There are only five or six, but their aggregate value is immense; he having given 35000 dollars for Dexter and I think 40,000 for Startle. He also when Startle's dam was in foal gave 5000 dollars for the foal that was in her. However the mare died with the foal inside her. Mr Bonner with his son and brother were cordial and pleasant; and shewed us everything. The first named is the greatest enthusiast I ever saw and he lectured us for near an hour on horses low down in the twenties, and waggons and sulkies and tracks till I at least began to think of breakfast.

Opposite Dexter he had the only produce of the famous Flora Temple—at least so I understood him—a colt called Prince. No trotter gets his speed or rather his best speed till he is nine years old, and they improve after that. Of course the blood is all originally English, crossed sometimes with what is called the Canadian trotting blood—that is blood originally imported from France by the first Canadian settlers.

This cut up the day very much and I did nothing but take a fast walk to the New York Club and take Tarbat to the Duncans for presentation. I dined with Stewart at a room which he shares with Boucicault over a restaurant in Fifteenth Street. There were pesent Hurlbert, Sam Ward, Boucicault, Chief Justice Shea, Mr O'Gorman, a man with a name something like Scaich.

Afterwards we went to the meeting of the Democratic party at the Manhattan Club. It was to celebrate their recent victorious elections. Imagine the tearoom of a ball with liveried attendants, and, standing round the room or grouped by the doors thirty or forty gentlemen. The president of the Club standing by the refreshments would say "I have now the pleasure to introduce to you Mr So and So": on which Mr So and So would step forward into the room and make a speech of five or ten minutes. In many cases no introduction or working up was required, it was the Bird of Freedom[1] at once. I heard Senator Bayard, Mr Cox member of Congress for New York, Mr Thayer, our convive Mr O'Gorman who was in terrific form and denounced the Cæsarism that lurked in the air, and ex-Governor Cleveland an old fashioned old gentleman in swallow tails. The speaking was very much above the average, while it would have been impossible for an Englishman without anything to hide his legs to speak at all.

Saturday Nov 15.
BREVOORT HOUSE, New York—milder weather.

Today Stuart conducted Tarbat, Allen and myself over the Herald office. It did not impress me so much as I had expected, partly because the work was not going on and partly because it did not bear being seen after Harper's.

The circulation is about ninety thousand copies a day.

After this we went to a lodging house for newsboys where they get a dinner for five cents and a bed for five cents. It was very clean and comfortable and has a little gymnasium and theatre. Most of the boys are Irish: and so was the kind hearted zealous Superintending Priest.

It is through such men that the Catholic Church obtains its hold over the poorer classes of the community. The boys are said to act very well: and I mean to try and see their performance.

After this we lunched at Sutherland's where I found Uncle Sam, who dragged me off to every sort of mercantile office. We also went into an old bookshop in Nassau Street, and finally walked home.

He and I dined with Hurlbert. There were also present Sidney Webster, Wilkie Collins, Lawrence Oliphant & Stuart. The dinner was very merry and lasted till past midnight, one of uncle Sam's most elaborate and erratic anecdotes lasting about an hour, and

1. The speeches may have attributed the election results to the behaviour of the American eagle.

finally breaking down completely on cross examination. However he revenged himself by falling ostentatiously asleep during a narrative of Stuart's of almost equal length.

Sunday Nov 16.

BREVOORT HOUSE, New York—a fine day.

This morning Duncan, Aleck Duncan, Miss Adèle, Miss Jessie and I all started by steamer for Randall's Island and Ward's Island whereon are situated the prisons penitentiaries, poorhouses and hospitals of New York.

The first institution we entered was a great refuge for homeless children. Everything was clean and comfortable. There was a large hospital attached to it. The large mass of children come here afflicted with some sort of ophthalmia, owing to their having lived in cellars and suchlike places. Then there is an asylum building for little idiots, all of them hopeless cases. One child seemed singularly bright: she was a little French girl and she could hardly be got to eat. In spite of her brightness her mind was beyond redemption. There are about 700 children in this institution including schools, hospitals and asylums.

Then we saw a curious hospital for inebriates, in which there are about 400 inmates. A charming neat matron shewed us over the place with the physician, who is privately supposed to be a drunkard himself. There are some charming rooms for which thirty dollars a week including board, washing and medical attendance are paid. These apartments have been occupied by a married couple and their baby. The husband would not go in without his wife and the wife would not go in without her baby. Another room was pointed out to me as having been occupied by two brothers who were drunkards. No case, as far as I could as certain, had yet turned out a permanent cure.

Then we went to the lunatic asylum. A huge building to commence with containing the harmless mad people: a painful not a horrible sight. Then a strong separate mansion for the violent cases. Here only Duncan and I went with Mr Gillman (an architect who had joined us).

This edifice gave a good elementary idea of hell. We passed down a passage, where through iron bars we saw hideous faces, expressing sullen ferocity, or maudlin tears or violent anger. Then one would begin to howl, and the contagion would spread and from every cell all round the building would be heard screams and roars and impotent curses. I asked the warden a stalwart good looking young Irishwoman if she were not afraid. "No, we do not dare to be afraid, leastways to shew we are. They use us terrible bad sometimes, drag us along the floor by our heads till we have hardly a hair left"; which was obviously an opening for me to compliment her on a very fine head of hair she had. There was yet a worse building, I found out afterwards.

Some of these poor mad women (they are all women here) have apparently lost their wits over religion. One had placed herself in the attitude of one of the old pictures of the Virgin in a benign attitude of prayer at the top of the great flight of steps, and remained fixed while we passed. Another was a thin piteous Mother of God. "They must all come back to their Mother" she said with cold conviction: much as the Pope and Henry the Fifth say to mankind. "They must all come back to their mother" with such simple earnestness that I began to agree with her that we were mad, and she alone was sane. Then she offered us diamonds "You may not want them, but they may come in useful for paying your fare". One of our party who was exceedingly pale and unhealthy looking she informed that he was not long for this world: which almost came with the force of an unpleasant probability.

But why this insanity about religion? Has religion driven them to madness, or have they, being mad, taken to religion?

After this we lunched and then moved on to the poorhouse. Here in huge separate buildings were 1365 helpless poor of both sexes. They are about equally divided as to sex, and the sexes are kept apart. One old couple we saw about eighty years each of them. Every day the old husband leaves the Male building and comes and spends a couple of hours with his wife embracing her and enquiring after her with the most tender solicitude. As they sat wagging, their ancient heads together, the old lady saw two of our party opposite her, and immediately announced "He is my husband you know sir" as if to prevent any suspicion of impropriety! Then we went to the prison, where there are 723 prisoners whose terms are five years and less, and whose costume is hideous flannel with stripes (or 'hoops' as they say on the turf) which gives them a terrible and zebra-like appearance. We saw them trooping into church. The Protestant service is in the afternoon and the Catholick in the morning, but many go to both in order to get out of their cells. All the cooking and baking is done by the prisoners. I asked the Governor if he thought any prisoner had ever left the jail a better man than he entered it? "It is very doubtful" he replied. Then we passed on to the shorter-period prison—a prison for short terms of ten days. It is a vast hall—the entire height of the building with cells on each side in stories up to the roof. All the prisoners were in church.

The last institution visited was the great hospital holding 1000 beds and at present 770 patients—as to sex about equally divided.

There were some painful syphilitic wards, containing with others persons who had received it by descent.

There was a ward for women 'near their time'. Eight out of ten of the children thus born were illegitimate. To judge by the ladies who were in this interesting condition, one may assert that no woman need despair of a lover.

And so we steamed back in a glorious afternoon of sunshine to New York. I ought to have mentioned that there were with us Commissioner Laimbeer of the Board of Charities and Correction which supervises these institutions and Mr Gillman an architect.

In the evening the Duncans, Senator Thurman of Ohio, Sam Ward and I set out to hear Ward Beecher at Brooklyn.

I am so dreadfully behindhand with my journal that I can give no detailed account of this very interesting scene.

The Church holds about 3000 people. We were accommodated in Mr Beecher's pew, where sat his wife a noble looking old lady, and the one behind it. There is an enormous organ on each side of which are places for the choir. In front of the organ is a dais with a table a desk and a chair. On the table is a tall flower glass containing lilies and other flowers. A similar glass is on the dais. At 7.30 Mr Beecher wearing a short opera cloak and holding a wideawake hat slipped into his chair, and sat for five minutes while the organ played a voluntary.

The service began with an anthem which lasted about seven minutes, then came a prayer, then a hymn, then a short portion of the Bible, then a hymn, then the sermon, then a prayer and then a final hymn sung to the dear tune of the Russian national anthem.

Beecher's sermon had two texts and five headings and lasted one hour. The five headings were written on a large sheet of paper, otherwise the sermon seemed extempore. At the end he launched out into a manifesto on Cuba, the whole of which he read with some difficulty from a manuscript.

I was greatly disappointed with him. The sequence of his headings was to say the least obscure, his manner was forced and artificial, his headings were neither developed nor argued out. Nor was I struck with his power over his congregation. It did not strike me as in any way equal to Spurgeon's. Twice indeed did the audience give him a round of clapping in his allusions to Cuba. But I was enabled to test his power in a very simple way. The same incident happened during sermon that occurred during Spurgeon's when I heard the latter, and in precisely the same way. A man was taken with a fit and carried out of church. Beecher used almost the same words as Spurgeon. "It is only one who is subject to these fits and will be removed in a moment". But it was easy to see how considerably the attention of the audience was diverted.

At one period he went off into a description of himself. "As to this little garden patch of mine" he said tapping the top of his head, "all that it has done is due to the cultivation of my parents and myself" and so on. Again, "Every drop of blood that flows in these veins is artizan blood—I say it not in boast" and so on. He ridiculed equality: "What makes a man in this world is nothing but brain", which struck me as a Pagan sentiment.

He is a buffoon without the merits of a buffoon. He has neither force nor ornateness of diction. His disdain for the graces of style was what perhaps impressed me most in his favour. But it is barely a merit of itself. At the same time a man, who is reputed an orator and a prophet, and does not mind repeating a word half a dozen times in a sentence has a certain *im*moral courage.

After the sermon I was introduced to him, and in conversation he impressed me more favourably. His countenance is not unpleasing: he has a broad sensual mouth and a high narrow forehead.

Sam Ward's behaviour was unctuous and edifying in the highest degree, and at supper, which we took afterwards at the Duncans' he announced that he had once read the burial service over forty three friends in a seavoyage. This we solemnly believed.

Altogether this was a day of many new emotions, more certainly than I can here set down.

Monday Nov 17.

BREVOORT HOUSE, New York—cold.

I called on Commissioner Laimbeer today at his office where he made me an oration on myself.

I dined with Stewart (*really O'Flaherty—who fled from trial in Great Britain) and Tarbat, John Sutherland (the restaurateur) and Sam Ward were the other guests. Afterwards we went to Niblo's and behind the scenes. There was a cloud of elderly houris, the principal and oldest of whom Miss Pauline Markham greatly attracted Tarbat. Luckily for him she eloped two or three days afterwards to Texas with an admirer.

It was raining a sort of wet snow when we came out. Romping in the carriage, one side of it came out, which was a novelty. Some might have thought the driver had a claim for damages, but Sam turned the tables on the wretched man by saying he could only pay him half fare after such a diabolical attempt to murder his passengers.

Tuesday Nov 18.

BREVOORT HOUSE, New York—bitter cold and slushy.

Today I went with commissioner Laimbeer to the Tombs police court. There were three magistrates sitting in what are called special police sessions. This court, intermediary between the general sessions and the ordinary police court, sits thrice a week and takes cognisance of 'penitentiary' offences—those which do not end in the State prison. I heard one or two cases decided.

Striking a horse with an iron shovel, prisoners pled guilty, one month in the penitentiary.

Two men, adulterating milk, pled guilty, fined 50 dollars each.

Then there was an Irish case of assault brought by a woman against a man. Of course the evidence shewed that the woman committed the assault, not the man.

Then there was an interesting case of petty larceny. A lad was hard up and stole something belonging to his master. The magistrates tried hard to make the employer forgive the boy, but the master was obdurate. Now what struck me in all the cases was this: the magistrates in dealing with these petty offences seemed to think much more of the future, the good or evil destiny, the possible improvement of young fellows who had committed their first offence than of the punishment. "What will he do when he gets out of prison, if we sentence him?" they ask each other. "What chance or certainty of employment have you if we let you off? How do you mean to gain your living?" they asked the prisoner. The whole scene (I have not recorded all the causes I heard decided) left on my mind a very pleasing impression.

Hurlbert, Allen, Ward, Tarbat and I dined together at the Brevoort.

Wednesday Nov 19.

BREVOORT HOUSE, New York—fine but cold.

This morning early I started with Tarbat and Stuart to see the

Girls' normal School. It contains a thousand pupils who go through a three years course and who enter at the average age of fifteen. We found all the pupils in the chapel singing, and very prettily they sang. Then we went into all the class rooms, where the abstruseness of the subjects, of instruction made my hair stand on end. At leaving I gave the president my card (hoping to call again), which I persuaded Tarbat was a greenback for sixty cents or half a crown, a present dictated by the usage of the country.

Afterwards Hurlbert took me to call upon the Barlows. After that again I telegraphed to Mary[1] my congratulations on her birthday.

I went with the Duncans and Senator Thurman to the opera. 'Il Travatore' was rather well performed and would have been enjoyable but for the chattering in the box.

Thursday Nov 20.

BREVOORT HOUSE, New York—fine by cold.

Today accompanied by Senator Thurman or rather accompanying Senator Thurman and the great A. Stewart himself I went over Stewarts Retail Drygoods Store. Stewart began with the legendary half crown, he now employs three thousand people in New York, one of his assistants he addressed as Judge, another as Major. This retail store has fifteen acres of flooring, he has mills in England Ireland and Scotland to feed his business here, Grant appointed him Secretary of the Treasury, and he can take up any articles in the whole shop-palace and tell you its cost. He is a thin precise looking man with a mouth like the slit in a money box.

Afterwards I went with Hurlbert to the Free College where a course of five years is given to certificated youths who have been at least a year in one of the public schools. Only about forty pass through the entire course out of about five hundred who begin. We spent a couple of hours there with great interest. One thing

1. His sister.

struck me. We saw a lad in a large hall standing alone in a somewhat artificial attitude. It turned out he was being taught the pose and gestures with which he was to deliver his "oration" of five minutes before the rest of the college.

I was greatly struck with the way in which Webb managed his army and with some little interviews he had with the lads, after schooltime.

One young man was troubling them all. He had passed first in the five years. He was now going in a special class of five for civil engineering. His receptivity was more than sufficient for what they could teach. In fine they could hardly supply him with sufficient straw for all the bricks he could make. Yet he was a blacksmith, and after the hours of study would shoe horses for the rest of the afternoon. Nature has her own little house of peers. And what peers!

I dined with Stewart at Sutherland's. The company was Sutherland himself, Tarbat, Jennings editor of the 'New York Times', Boucicault, S. S. Cox member of Congress for New York, and ultimately Judge O'Sullivan of Samana Bay who was drunker than Judges should be. He was so much behind the scenes of English society that he knew that neither I or any English gentleman could be seen at Baron Rothschild's dinner table without disgrace or indeed at all. The Prince of Wales indeed has dined there but he could and would do anything.

I followed O'Sullivan to the Smoking room of the Brevoort, where he ordered champagne, and where I found Thomson the Canadian member for Welland and a friend. I asked Thomson many questions about the recent phases of Canadian politics to which he would only answer "Read my address to my constituents you will find it all there". At last he announced to me that he had taken a great fancy to me at Ottawa from observing the shape of my head, upon which without further ado, he laid violent hands. It was a curious sight in an American smoking room at 2 a.m.: a young fellow in the hands of a muscular Canadian proclaiming revelations of his subject's character to O'Sullivan snoring and drunk and a remonstrating friend.

Friday Nov 21.

BREVOORT HOUSE, New York—cold but fine.

Today from having made appointments with Sam Ward which that hero failed to keep, my entire day was muddled away. I dined and went to the Opera with the Duncans'. The opera was Rigoletto, not well sung but tolerably acted.

Saturday Nov 22—a lovely day.

Today I left New York for Boston in company (Sam having thrown me over) with Duncan and his daughter and niece. Prescott provided me with a magnificent room at the Somerset Club, and I dined with Winthrop, P. The Duncans and Miss Thayer an inarticulate daughter of Mrs Winthrop's.

After dinner Duncan and I strolled for a few minutes into the Howard Athenæum, a sort of Alhambra or Niblo on a very small scale. There was a very good female gymnast and some amusing negroes.

Sunday Nov 23.

SOMERSET CLUB, Boston—fine but cold.

Sam arrived this morning with Tarbat whom he at once packed off to church with Duncan.

He and I drove off to breakfast at noon with Longfellow and his three unmarried daughters. We had a very pleasant visit, remaining two or three hours. Longfellow is a noble and serene old man with long white hair and a white beard. He inhabits a house which Washington made his headquarters for a short time, and which he describes in "Hyperion", p. 294.

Afterwards we drove to South Boston to see Sam's sister Mrs Julia Ward Howe, a well known lecturer on female rights. She was at home with a handsome daughter, and though reputed very learned, singularly soft and feminine and charming. To see Sam with her and hear him as usual announcing the occasional inconveniences he found in being a Buddhist from the difficulty of communicating with his grand Lama was very funny.

I dined with the Prescotts. There was Mr and Mrs Prescott, Miss Edith Prescott a charming girl with a frank eye, the dear 'little Hero' Linsee, Longfellow and his daughter Edith, Charles Sumner who most goodnaturedly brought me the last English paper, and Mrs. Lawrence. The little Hero sat most demurely through dinner and looked ten Solomons in one.

We had a 'very good time'—admirable expression but I think we were a little overweighted (at least I was) with our big guns. How happy could we have been with either, had t'other dear charmer remained away.

Afterwards Longfellow went to shew himself at Winthrop's and took me with him. He is admirably unaffected. The only two new faces there were Messrs Swette and Rotch. I walked home with the latter.

Monday Nov 24.

SOMERSET CLUB, Boston—a rainy and somewhat damnable day.

After harassing myself all night for fear I should not be called, I rose at six. No tea to be had, nothing but housemaids and draughts. Duncan called for me at seven and carried my remains to the station. We arrived at Providence at 9.30. It is a picturesque hilly neat little smug town, but has 80,000 inhabitants and more and is going ahead. Duncan did business and I wrote letters till 12 when we started to see the Ashton mills, a few miles out of the city. It is a fine mill with forty two thousand spindles, four hundred and fifty hands and English machinery with all the modern improvements. But of this in my notebook. We were shown the mill by young

Gammell a pleasant friendly lad with deep sunk eyes—the heir to his grandfather Ives' enormous fortune.

It poured all day. We visited in the afternoon the old Duncan house, just sold, a large wooden house on a noble site, where Duncan's father long lived. Thence to the Butler Lunatic Asylum founded by Duncan's great uncle from whom he got his name and this large Providence property. There are 124 patients here. One of them, whom we saw, Mr Reed, is worth a million dollars. He broke into Nilsson's room and demanded her in instant marriage. He is now planning a spiral railway which he explained to me at some length under an oath of secrecy.

We also went over the Butler Exchange, a great building for shops, which Duncan has just built. It cost 70,000 £ and ought to pay £12,000 annual rent.

We passed a Quaker College. How I should like to have seen it.

We dined with Mr Moses Goddard a member of the great predominant Ives family and being who are to Providence what the Peases are to Darlington. He plumes himself on his soap and champagne—justly as regards the latter.

We afterwards visited Mr Ives the old millionaire head of the firm. He is worth two millions sterling, and we found him in his seventy seventh year, alone in a dimly lighted room with a full length portrait of his only child, a son killed in the war the last of his name. Who shall say that riches are everything?

He seemed a man who interested himself in the outside world.

On returning to the hotel we were greeted by a leading citizen Mr Henry Lippett. Mr Lippett was in his cups. He took us for a drink by main force. "What will you have—say—hot Scotch—say—that's your national drink—say—you wont'? You look so damned innocent but you must have a drink sometimes—say we have a big thing on our hands—say—I'll tell you what we mean to do we mean to take Cuba—you look so cold blooded—say—ain't you interested—I'll tell you what it is, the English government is chawed up—there's nothing but Lords and people—say—there's no English government". As he waited for an answer I said that I had just seen an English newspaper a fortnight old by which it

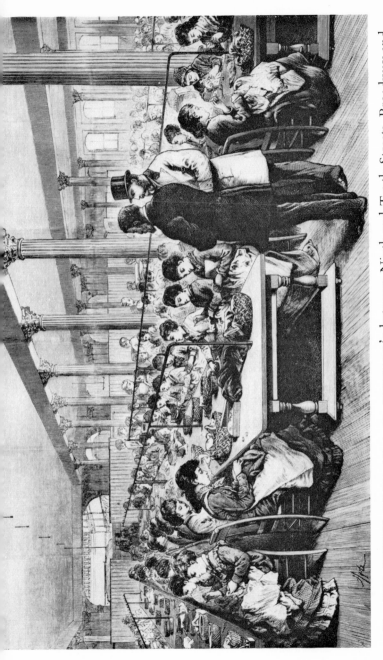

VI. THE SEWING-ROOM AT A. T. STEWART'S between Ninth and Tenth Streets, Broadway and Fourth Avenue

VII. FAST TROTTERS ON HARLEM LANE

appeared that the English government was still—though in its old wretched way—rubbing on. Perhaps he had had later telegrams? "Yes, I've had later telegrams—say—Willie Duncan don't you agree with me—say—Willie Duncan you're not going to turn round on our little institutions" etc. etc. etc. He was by far the most amusing Drunkard I ever saw. We had however to go off to the station, and the last words I heard in the good town of Providence were these "By Jesus Christ you don't know where the bloody hell you're going to". I did not know the speaker, but I thought he was a quaint citizen of Providence.

I ought to mention that the Ives faction all openly (except the old man) triumphed in the ruin of the Spragues not merely as a rival house but because Senator Sprague had most wantonly attacked the old man's dead son in Congress after his death. Still the Goddard triumph was horribly rancorous.

We left Providence at 11 p.m. and arrived in New York at 6 a.m.

Tuesday Nov 25.

BREVOORT HOUSE, New York—fine and mild.

I slept for two or three hours—from 6.30 to 9.30. After breakfast I walked down town to get some money—with Ward. King the banker explained to me their curious safe lock capable of a hundred million variations. Then I gave Ward luncheon at Sutherland's

All Broadway was decorated with the Stars and Stripes for Nov 25 is "Evacuation day"—the day on which the British troops marched out of New York "and the Irish marched in" as the Englishman remarked in the story.

I never saw Broadway look so lovely as it did with the evening lights from the distant sunset just catching the tops of the houses and the streaming flags.

There was a review in front of the City Hall. I had been introduced to Mayor Havemeyer and my card procured Ward and myself good places on the steps. It was a curious sight to see the stout and elderly Mayor with a man on one side of him bearing an eagle on a staff and on the other a man carrying the banner of the Mayoralty and followed by such aldermen as could be found walking up and down the line of soldiers. The regiment was a crack regiment—the seventh New York—which supplied I was told 500 officers to the U.S. army during the rebellion. It was then under the command of General Duryce who was present today. The march past was very well done and the men were very fine physical specimens. One was a big fleshy grandson of General Winfield Scott. The men are excused jury duty while in the corps; while in it they are drilled once a week for six months of the year and are subject to military law.

Afterwards I went for a moment to the office of the editor of the Scottish-American Journal—a courteous and intelligent man called Stewart.

Afterwards I dined with the Barlows at 1, Madison Square. A most cheery dinner which began with maccaroni manufactured by Miss Elsie Barlow and an Italian gentleman who was dining there.

Hurlbert, who was dining there too, and I remained till the unnatural hour of 11 (which is very late here) and then had roast oysters and hock at the Manhattan Club.

Wednesday Nov 26.—cold.

Breakfasting late, I did not accomplish much today. I bought books at Appleton's, which was my principal feat.

I gave dinner to Evarts, Rothery, Hurlbert and Ward. Evarts was singularly agreeable. Somebody said Snooks had committed suicide. 'He is too lazy' said Hurlbert. "He might manage it in a recumbent position" said Evarts.

Duncan came in afterwards, and that and Sam's letting fall a bottle of his own choicest madeira which he had contributed with a wild turkey to the feast, were the principal events. The feast was at Delmonico's.

We afterwards i.e. R. Russell, Balfour, Ward and I made a descent on Watson's hell, finding Sam Ward gliding into Morrissey's purgatory alongside. We did not remain long, and finished the evening with oysters at the Traveller's.

Thursday Nov 27. Thanksgiving Day.
BREVOORT HOUSE, New York—a fine mild day.

Today we went a large party under Duncan to his villa in Staten Island, and there shot pigeons. In the first sweep I was left in alone with the winner Lauderdale Duncan, but missed my seventh or eighth bird. I then missed two more in other sweeps and went home. It was a pleasant day, we had a cheery party—all men—and a roaring luncheon.

I dined with the Duncans—Thanksgiving dinner—Turkey and Cranberry sauce and Pumpkin pie. After dinner looked over Miss Jessie's collection of autographs. She has a good collection (which I weeded of some titled nobodies) containing as the gems of what part I saw long letters from John Winthrop and Roger Williams, and Daniel Webster's notes for the termination of his famous speech of March 7, 1850. To bed at 11.

Friday Nov 28.
BREVOORT HOUSE, New York—fine.

All today was muddled away—partly by my being idiot enough to make appointments with young Englishmen, partly from the schools being shut from yesterday till Monday and finally from the illtemper resulting from these minor misfortunes.

I however concluded my purchases at Appleton's and ordered the parcel to be sent off.

I dined with the Duncans for the opera. There were only a ratt-
ling cheery Mr Parker and Balfour. The opera was 'Aida' which
was wonderfully well put on the stage.

Saturday Nov 29.

BREVOORT HOUSE, New York—bright.

Today Rothery, Evarts and I went to hear Judge Davis pass
sentence on Graham Bartlett, Fullerton and their three junior
counsel for contempt of court.

Fullerton read a long written defence and then Davis began. I
could hardly have wished a word or a gesture altered. What he did
most skilfully was this that while in studiously moderate language
he fined the three I have named 250 dollars each, he only admon-
ished the three juniors, contriving by his advice to them to admin-
ister the most telling backhanders at their principals. He made one
ludicrous slip; speaking of two of these young men he said that
during this trial they had given proof of "no *uncommon*
abilities".

The court was crowded, and evidently sympathised with the
Judge. After the judgment the fine was paid and we went. Graham
one of these counsel dresses and arranges his hair like a roundhead.
I never saw such a figure.

I afterwards went to my bankers for some money and then
walked home.

I dined tête à tête with Hurlbert at his club, after accompanying
the Barlows and Miss Gandy to a 'kettledrum' at the Kings'. A
kettledrum is a sort of drum at four oclock in the afternoon. I soon
went away, escorting Miss Barlow to some house where she wished
to visit.

After dinner commissioner Laimbeer called for me and took me
to the Tombs. Thence Warden Johnson and I set out with a
detective to see the night side of that part of New York. First we
went to see what one would call the casual ward of the police
office, where in one room were sixty six men and in another about

twenty women who had come in for shelter. Anyone has a right to
come in at this time of year, but no food is given. In the police
office there was a cheerful collection of knives and choppers and
pistols that had committed innumerable murders and suicides,
called the 'deodand' collection.

Then we surveyed the 'five points' formerly the Seven Dials of
New York. Formerly there stood here an old brewery deserted
by all but thieves and harlots: when pulled down, many skeletons
were found in the vats and privies. Now the 'Five Points' is much
reformed.

We dashed down a dark passage through a breakneck causeway
thence into a hole which led into a cellar crowded with little shoeblacks and newsboys. Some older lads were acting and singing
nigger songs and dancing nigger dances. These were older shoeblacks who lived entirely by these performances, each taking a
benefit in turn. The charge for admission was five cents. We had
seats given us on the rude stage and kept one eye on the performance, and the other on the audience. One of the latter was so bright
and cheery that it seemed horrible he should grow into a thief, so
I sent for him when we had gone out, got his name and some
particulars about him from the kind detective, and told him to
come and black my boots next morning. As if I had not enough
duties and encumbrances without saddling myself with Patrick
Shea!

Thence into a Chinese gambling house where some members of
that favoured nation sat round a table playing what appeared to be
dominoes, but which was nothing of the kind. They declined to
let us risk five cents, as we did not know the game. In the other
room was a gentleman who was both priest and hellkeeper—
functions apparently incompatible but which I have often known
united in Calvinistic ministers. In the centre of his room, quite
convenient, was his deity. It consisted in a table on which was a
cup of tea without milk or sugar, two stuffed birds under glass
cases, a jar of incense and two glass candlesticks. All this was in
front and in honour of the portrait of a gentleman strongly
resembling the late commissioner Yeh. Over the portrait were

crossed two peacock's feathers. Round about on the walls were long papers covered with Chinese characters, containing I was told the list of members of the congregation and the accounts of the gambling house. It was very instructive but I did not like to examine things very closely, out of tenderness for the priest who stood by and who was extremely angry with a little Chinaman for answering a question. In the gambling room there was another little portrait with another cup of tea, but that was all.

Thence to an interminable series of dancing houses: all doing a somewhat dull business because of the badness of the times. In one kept by a man called George Christopher there was no dancing but a girl singing an interminable history of some naval engagement. Our detective had formerly arrested her as drunken when a man whom he had afterwards discovered to be her brother tried to beg her off as it was her first offence. She came of respectable parents, and the brother being respectable too would not own the relationship, so the detective arrested her and here she was.

In the regular dancing places the girls were in a sort of ballet costume. They were all fiends I was told—outwardly they certainly were: women who would decoy men up to their rooms, rob them of everything nor stick at a bit of knifework if required.

Perhaps the worst place we saw was a drinking place called the Velvet House, with a crowd of thieves in the room and a little shut off closet where there were huddled together six or eight of the most horrible looking women I ever saw; one was stretched under the bench like a bunch of old clothes, and was fished up cursing by the policemen. They sat there, waiting till a man was drunk enough to be put into their vulture cage. Everybody knew our detective D'Orsey, and he knew everybody.

Then we went to visit a villanous looking negro called Jack Spicer. His wife a white woman sat there with a whitlow on her thumb, while a woman cleaned the house. Mrs Spicer said that being ill she had asked "this lady" to assist us. It sounded very funny. Mr Spicer was obdurate tonight and declined to shew us anything.

I was taken to a 'double alley' in Cherry Street, where it was calculated that in every house of four windows there were lodged from sixty to seventy families.

We ended our survey (of which all this is a very mild hurried description) in the Bowery at two German *cafés chantants*. In one the orchestra consisted of young decent looking girls dressed in pink, who played very well. This was a respectable place. It pays I believe wonderfully well, though all the profit would appear to be on the lager beer; for there is no entrance fee. However I am told that the percentage of profit on lager beer is something incredibly large.

There we took leave of our detectives and the Warden and I wandered home looking into various places of amusement on our way in a sort of Tom and Jerry[1] way, without seeing anything very interesting.

Sunday Nov 30. St Andrew's Day.

BREVOORT HOUSE, New York—very cold.

I went with the Duncans to hear Mr Brooks preach at Grace-church. He preached an excellent sermon full of vitality and courage, on the positive and negative manner of leading a Christian life and overcoming our sinful natures. From the word positive having been used repeatedly during the sermon it happened that a lady hearer expressed to me the pleasure she had felt at Mr Brooks' admirable sermon on Positivism.

At half past three I was bidden to dine with A. T. Stewart in his new marble palace, but we did not sit down to dinner till half past four: as we looked through his gallery of pictures which contains the 'Horse Fair' by Rosa Bonheur, and one of the originals of Power's Greek Slave. There was a picture, just bought, small, and unframed, by Carl Bierstadt of a longly rock on the Californian coast which stuck me very much the rock is covered with gulls and

1. See Pierce Egan: *Life in London; or the day and night scenes of Jerry Hawthorn Esq., and his elegant friend Corinthian Tom;* 1821.

with sea lions quite at their ease and unconscious of humanity while a great Pacific wave is bringing up another sealion with a fish in his mouth. It is real savage solitude.

Our company was composed of the Rotherys, Judge Hilton Mr Stewart's right hand man, Mr Swann an English barrister, Mr Leary, Mr Stewart's niece and an anonymous gentleman.

The dinner was long and elaborate served apparently from Delmonico's, though the wines were my host's pride: and as I sat on his left hand he took almost too much care to have my forest of glasses filled and refilled. All the house appears lined and floored with marble. We did not dine in the palatial dining room but in a small adjacent parlour.

Miss Stevens to whom I had engaged myself by mistake to dine today, declined to let me off and insisted on my coming there from Stewart's. So I left Stewart at seven and found Mrs and Miss Stevens entertaining Miss Wadsworth and Miss Beckwith (both beauties) and Messrs Jay, Kane and Newbold.

People came in after dinner very much in the foreign fashion. They were chiefly Englishmen who displayed, considering they were strangers in the country astonishing moral courage, I thought.

Monday Dec 1. New York—snow.

I called on Mr Wood this morning who was lately one of the commissioners of Schools and had a long talk with him. Afterwards I drove down town and had a talk with the good Father Drumgoole of the St Vincent de Paul about Patrick Shea, who never came yesterday by the bye, but came this morning with the detective. I found him as usual in the midst of his shoeblacks working away as bright and as happy as an angel. He expressed himself delighted to help me. "I have given my life" he said "to these little fellows. It is astonishing how much good there is in them, how much willingness to be good."

In the evening I attended the St Andrews' dinner. I arrived late, and found all the members walking arm in arm to dinner. This enabled me to join a party at a round table in the corner consisting of Balfour, McKerrell, Tarbat, Romilly etc. At last however I was fetched away to the dais by one of the vice presidents in spite of all remonstrances. There I was placed between General Arthur (*afterwards President) collector of Customs a pleasant jovial man: and an old Mr. Irving also jovial but deaf as a post. He enquired of me categorically the exact incomes of different members of the peerage, and when I refused further information from combined weariness and ignorance said with a chuckle "we in America think many of our merchants quite as rich as the English peers". On which I assured him that that was a fact but that things had much changed since he left Scotland and that we in Britain thought very little of mere money now. Heaven forgive me. At an early stage of the dinner I saw that many had already celebrated the anniversary and that the rest were determined to do so very fully: the air was stifling moreover. When the whole three hundred Scots lit cigars and began puffing into the disturbed air, I thought I should have given up the ghost.

The first toast was "The day and all who honour it": the second "The Queen": the third "The President": the fourth "The Land O'Cakes". To this replied a Scotch minister of a most pronounced type, and when I heard the well known accent, and saw the wonted shake of the polemical pow I knew my fate. For five and twenty minutes did that excellent divine with perfect satisfaction to himself discourse about Scott and Burns and hills and lakes and Robert the Bruce and would be orating now if ominous signs had not shown that some of the company had heard this sort of thing before and would not stand it again. In Scotland, we should have cheered and wept for hours, but here the reverend Thomson had to sit down. After this I sneaked away suffocated to the opera where Nilsson sang the 'Huguenots' very well. Then I returned to Delmonico's to fetch Balfour from the dinner. From upstairs proceeded howls, down the stairs was being borne a man insensibly drunk, not by any means the first. R. Russell and I waited in the restaurant for half an hour. At last new thunders were heard: the

4*

revellers were coming down. The doors were hastily shut and peace gradually returned. McKerrell whom I had never before known to be a favourite of the Muses had sung two songs. Oh Scotland what crimes are committed in thy name!

After this we went to Jimmy Watson's as by previous appointment. Rothery was to have come but did not. Baccarat was the game at which Russell displayed courage and talent enough to dissipate the fortune of a Rothschild.

Tuesday Dec 2.

BREVOORT HOUSE, New York—somewhat damnable. Wet snow on the ground and a drizzling rain.

Today was an impossible day. I had an immense deal of packing to do what with sending a coffin full of books to England and going to Washington myself. I called on Miss Beckwith in the afternoon and found Judge Pierce (I think) there. I dined with the Duncans where Mr Henry Duncan, Mrs Duncan's brother in law, and Mr Sargent her nephew with his bride Miss Robeson that was. After dinner I started for Washington: I could not open the window of my section and the heat was stiffling, so much so that I dressed myself at two o'clock in the morning and went out to breathe air. It was a pleasant morning as we approached Washington, and it was a grand sight when from some distance I saw the great white dome of the Capitol rising pure and splendid from a cloud, as it were: the base being wrapped in mist.

Wednesday Dec 3.

WELCHER'S HOTEL, Washington—a spring day soft and mild.

Sam Ward was waiting for me at the station like a dear old chap. I got capital rooms at Welcher's, and after breakfast we set out for the Capitol. I think Pennsylvania Avenue with the Capitol at one end and the Treasury at the other the finest street I have ever seen.

We went to the Assembly where Speaker Blaine gave me 'the floor' i.e. placed me on a chair on the right hand of the marble tribune in which he sits. One may also walk anywhere about the houes. Cox ('Sunset' Cox of New York) introduced me to Stevens of Georgia the ex-vice president of the Confederacy—a very old feeble looking man who has just taken his seat. I sat next to him for some time. Presently Cox brought up Butler to present me to, and at Butler's request I think introduced him to Stevens. I thought this sufficiently remarkable, Ben. Butler of New Orleans being presented to the Vice President of the Confederacy. They seemed quite friendly or rather civil. Butler had been presented to Stevens twenty years before which the latter had forgotten, but, as Butler remarked, "it was an event in *my* life Mr Stevens though nothing to you". Stevens talked to me a good deal about the Rebellion, but was not very audible in the din that prevailed. I was introduced to a good many other members, such as Mr Maynard of Tennessee who that evening received a "serenade".

I dined with Sam Ward at Welcher's. The other guests were Sir E. Thornton the British Minister, Mr Kasson member for Iowa, Senator Thurman the leader of the democratic party, C. A. Bristed who wrote "Five Years in an English University" which I remember reading at Eton, Senator Sumner, Professor Peirse of the Coast Survey, and Mr Donn Piatt the editor of the "Capitol" I think. We had a very pleasant evening. I sat between Sam Ward and Sumner.

Thursday Dec 4.

WELCHER'S HOTEL, Washington—very warm.

After breakfast Ward and I started for the Senate where Senator Conkling introduced me to a number of senators—Boutwell

the late secretary of the Treasury, Cameron chairman of the
Foreign Affairs Committee, Frelinghuysen, Carpenter a brilliant
fellow now labouring under a social accusation, Sherman the
colleague of Thurman from Ohio but a republican, Anthony
of Delaware and so on. I stayed some time while Senator Ferry of
Michigan read aloud a long speech on finance. This was hardly
pretended as a speech to the Senate: as soon as delivered it would
be printed and circulated among his constituents. It was interrupted by a man appearing with an envelope fully a foot square
with an enormous red seal like a letter in a pantomime, which
turned out to be a message from the president containing appointments. So as soon as the Michigan orator was "through", the
standing committees were read out, and the House went into
executive session which is always secret. Being thus expelled I went
to the House of Representatives which soon adjourned, so I walked
home. On my way home I called on Stevens of Georgia, where
a Colonel Alston told us some interesting stories of the late war,
but the room was so hot that I moved on.

Sam gave a second dinner tonight of infinite grandeur where
I dined and where there were, Robeson secretary of the Navy,
Attorney General Williams who has just been nominated Chief
Justice of the United States, Senator Conkling who has just refused
to be, Judge Field of the Supreme Court, senator Anthony,
General Garfield, Judge Hale and Mr Frye all in Congress, and
senator Bayard. Sam had composed a fancy bill of fare with a
soup à la Dalmeny and so forth. We remained, or rather a rump
of us, in the diningroom till near midnight when Sam and I walked
to Mrs Admiral Porter's "German" a party so called being a
cotillon with no other dancing. I found Mrs Porter sitting with
Mrs Thurman and the President (*Grant) in the supper room.
The President was soon afterwards, conducted like the prince of
Wales to have his smoke, and I was introduced to his daughter
Nellie and some other girls in a break of the dancing—the prettiest
of whom was Miss Paul (*afterwards Mrs Astor) of Philadelphia
—not yet out. I did not watch the 'German' long and when the
president came back I walked home with a German diplomatist

who told me some curious stories about Bismark whom he had
known at Frankfort in 1852 and ever since.

Friday Dec 5.
   WELCHER'S HOTEL, Washington—snowing.

After Uncle Sam and I had breakfasted we drove together to the
House of Representatives. The House is opened by a bang on the
Speaker's desk given by an auctioneer's hammer of enormous size:
then follows a prayer like one of the shorter prayers of a Presby-
terian minister i.e. a short address on the attributes of the Creator and
the functions of Congress. Then follows the reading for verification
or correction of the minutes of the previous sitting. This on the
present occasion took up an hour fully, a pure waste of time. Then
an hour of proposals and resolutions: then the moment of excitement—the reading out of the list of standing committees for the
session. This is as it were reading out the class list at Oxford, and
the greatest anxiety is felt all through the House even by the most
eminent men to know if they are to retain or mend their positions.
For instance Senator Sumner since his quarrel with the Republican
party and his expulsion from the chairmanship of the great Foreign
Affairs Committee of the Senate has now only two back places on
insignificant committees. In the senate these committees are
nominated by the two parties themselves in proportion to their
numbers. In the House of Representatives they are nominated
by the Speaker—a great possibly a dangerously great power.
Generals Butler and Hurlbert agreed that an unfair Speaker could
pass any bill he liked by the system pursued.
   As I did not expect to be nominated to any important committee
I contained my feelings. By the bye just before the reading out of
the committees a curious incident occurred. "The member for
New Mexico (I think) desires to make an explanation: is there
any objection?" To which there were simply cries of "How
Long?" To this pertinent enquiry put without any unnecessary

prefaces, the unhappy member at last answered "Two minutes".
But the directness, the almost cynical directness amused me.

The House now adjourned till Monday, so Sam and I returned
home, leaving a card at the White House on the way.

Sam and Generals Butler and Hurlbert dined with me. Ben
Butler is well known enough. His ugliness is startling. A head like
the head of an enormous snake, two ferociously squinting eyes
in bulbous caverns of corrugated skin, the end of his face passing
directly into his neck without the hollow form of a chin: one could
almost fancy seeing a rabbit projecting from it which he had
gorged, as is said to be the case with a boa constrictor. He was
extremely agreeable, the only drawback being that one has not the
remotest idea whether he is looking at you or out of the window.

General Hurlbert, brother of my friend, does not resemble
William Henry in the least. He is thin lean narrow with a high
peaked forehead giving one the idea of a captain in Harrison's
Fifth Monarchy regiment.

We had a charming evening. At the very beginning we formed
ourselves into a committee of iconoclasts. The result was awful:
among the debris one could recognise General Washington's
aggravating under lip and Ben Franklin's puffy chin, and I am
sorry to say that General Lee's effigy was torn out of my private
temple and violently thrown down. However it was not injured
and I at once put it up again immediately locking the door of my
sadly denuded shrine now a beggarly show of empty niches.

Saturday Dec. 6.

WELCHER'S HOTEL, Washington—very fine.

There, my first smudge, caused by running to the window to see
two negroes going out for a Sunday ride. My first business this
morning which I thought would be very simple was to buy some
"J" pens. However I asked at nine shops and found no pens of that
sort. In my search I walked as far as the Capitol.

After breakfast I set out with Sam and saw the Navy and Treasury departments. In the Treasury I was introduced to Secretary Richardson and Senator Morrill of Maine. I thought it was 'tariff Morrill" and said that I feared this interview of theirs boded no good to Free Trade. "No", they said, "there was no chance for Free Trade". I said that I thought they had ridden Mill's hesitating exception in their favour very hard. I could not help afterwards thinking what Gladstone would think if a young American were almost forcibly brought into his room of a morning and bantered him lightly on his budget!

We next called on a widow—Mrs Johnson—Sam's Stella I think. She using the word 'bore', I said that I did not know it was used in America. "O yes" she said "we use quite a number of English words". Good God! thought I, what is the language composed of then?

Next to Sam's lodging's. "Get out" said Sam's black coachman and Leporello to me "get out and have a drink with him". By the bye Sam's coachman is delightful. He said to Sam the other day "Dat very nice little gentleman, but tell me one thing, does he come from England or Europe". On the present occasion I followed his advice and the bottle had hardly been got out when in stalks John, "come Mr Ward ain't you going to give me a drink". Drink! Of course he was.

Then came in Sam's page, and rocked himself in silence and the most comfortable chair in the room. Finally we set out with senator Bayard, who took a glass of whiskey and water, to the Agricultural Bureau. Here we found Mr Watts the superintendent seated in his room behind samples of grain and preserved lobsters and peaches. Sam says "that poor fellow Watts he sits there all day hardly daring to look at the papers. Then he sees there is only a half crop in Vermont, and there are weevils in Ohio, and a fly in Maine and he tears his hair saying 'What on earth shall I put in my report, all this spoils my report'. We walked over the collection of stuffed birds noting a beautiful woodduck chiefly, and the collection of plants where Bayard and I racked our senses to find a sensitive plant pinching all the leaves we saw including hollies, while Sam lingered in poetical ecstasies over south american scrubs. Then off to call on Donn Piatt the editor of the Capitol, who has revenged himself by making fun of me in his next number. We dined at Sumner's—a charming party—Senator Carl Schurz, Caleb Cushing, marquis de Chambrun.

Sumner after dinner came out in the character of a virtuoso with Milton's autograph in an album which also contained Strafford's: and Burke's MS of the "Appeal from the New to the Old Whigs". If one could only believe in the autographs one buys. He had hung up in his dining room Franklin & C. J. Fox, and the famous Venetian picture of St Mark releasing the Christian slave of which he had made striking use in one of his orations, reciting me the passage. And he had a picture supposed to be Lely's portrait of the duchess of Cleveland, and had been taken to task for hanging up a king's mistress: most unjustly, for it is not the duchess of Cleveland nor is it by Sir Peter Lely. And he had the divine Neapolitan Psyche, whom none of these fastastic sect founders have ever had the sense to make their idol: out upon them! He kept me talking till near midnight, long after everybody else had gone, while Sam who had taken his leave at ten blandly read poetry in a distant room.

Sumner's house is the house of a virtuoso: it would take a week to look through his treasures.

Sam came to the hotel and 'discoursed' me till 1. AM.

Cushing and Schurz by the bye are both 'generals'.

Sunday Dec 7.

WELCHER'S HOTEL, Washington—mild.

One of the 'peculiar institutions' of Washington is the oyster seller. He goes round with oysters in a tin can, blowing a horn to announce himself. This however does not bear on Sunday Dec 7, except that on Sunday one hears him not.

After breakfast, Sam Ward and I set out for Baltimore, and on arriving (Baltimore is forty miles from Washington) we walked to the Cathedral which is a plain dome filled with pews but without much of the splendour of Catholicism; and thence to the Maryland Club. There we were greeted by Mr Otho Williams a very English looking gentleman, and by Mr Gilmor who is a Scottish Gilmour and proud of it.

Baltimore is called the Monumental City and is very proud of her monuments. She erected the first to Washington—a magnificent marble column bearing the inscription "George Washington by the State of Maryland", and the great man himself on the top with a lightning conductor sprouting from his brow. Close to this there was a very handsome Methodist Church of green marbles.

We dined at the Club. Just before dinner I was introduced to an elderly Weld of Lulworth who is drawn here by love of canvas back shooting. Mr Gilmor dined with us, and our dinner consisted of terrapin and canvas back alone. The gentle stirring of the terrapin, and the carving or rather tearing of the duck were beautiful to witness, for he performed both operations as labours of love. A canvas back is divided into four parts. The wing and leg are skilfully torn off together on each side, then the merrythought (which is the titbit) is torn from the carcase, and the remaining breast forms the fourth portion. But the worship of this grey wildfowl in Baltimore must be seen to be believed.

As we did not go by the 6.30 train we had to wait for the 4.20 a.m. train. We slept in an hotel with our clothes on.

Monday Dec 8.

WELCHER'S, Washington—fine and mild.

I went to bed on arriving, and slept sound till ten. I paid my usual visits to the Legislature. In the Senate a senator was as usual reading some essay aloud. In the House of Representatives after a roll call, I saw the Amnesty Bill passed almost by acclamation. Nothing now remains of the rebellion, except of course the great result of the Abolition of Slavery.

I had a long conversation with Cannon the Utah delegate, and walked home with 'Sunset' Cox the restless New York member.

Cox considers that his conduct on the Salary Grab question makes it certain that he will be nominated for the Vice Presidency.

I went down and sat with Sam Ward's dinner party—Mr David Wells, general Garfield, and Mr Orton—and afterwards went on to dine with Sir Edward Thornton at the British Legation. At dinner there were Secretary Fish, Senator Bayard, Howard, Capt Gore Jones, Mr Cantrell, Mr French and Mr Charlton of the Legation. We had a pleasant dinner and remained in the drawing room till the unheard-of hour of 11.45. After which Secretary Fish Senator Bayard and I walked home together.

Tuesday Dec 9.
WELCHER'S, Washington—mild and fine.

This morning I started for the State Department which, pending the building of the new offices, is situated in an Orphan Asylum. Secretary Fish had to leave at once for a cabinet so Mr Bancroft Davis shewed me over the rooms. There is here the original draught of the Declaration of Independence in Jefferson's handwriting; moreover all the Washington correspondence including a curious book containing his accounts and letters before the war, all kept in his own neat handwriting. One I noticed was a letter ordering his London tailor to send him clothes and telling the tailor in case the measure is lost that he is six feet high and proportioned for that height: he also orders breeches for Master Custis, his stepson, aged fourteen and tall of his age. The best portrait of Washington —that by Peel of Philadelphia—is here: those by Stewart are considered to have been very flattering.

After this I drove to the Capitol, to the top of which I mounted, and saw the fine view in the sunlight. Thence I went to the House of

Representatives and heard a vigorous debate on the Back Pay question. 'Sunset' Cox spoke, and then there was a vigorous member from Nevada and Judge Lawrence of Ohio who appears universally detested and was silenced by Wilson of Indiana. Meanwhile the members (and I among them) all crowded round and made a sort of ring in which Wilson and Lawrence contended. Altogether the scene was sufficiently turbulent. I was rather amused by Speaker Blaine's taking a huge apple off his table and walking out of the House with it, saying to me as he passed "Now I do insist on your saying when you get back to England that the Speaker of the House of Representatives when he wants to eat an apple goes to his own room to do it."

Sam Ward and I and Withers dined together at Welcher's, and afterwards went with Williamson the Attorney General's secretary to hear Mrs Julia Ward Howe lecture on "Men's women and Women's women". I was not greatly impressed by the lecture though I think Mrs Howe so pleasant in private life that I hardly like to write criticism on her.

After this Sam and Sunset Cox and I went off to a reception at Fernando Wood's. It was what the Americans call a "stag party" that is a party without ladies, but it was very pleasant. I was particularly glad to see General Sherman who owns I think the finest face I have seen in America: a grand forehead and an iron mouth and chin. Alexander H. Stevens was there, feeble as usual and in a velvet cap. He seemed to be the object of great attention and curiosity. Presently a supper buffet was thrown open at which there was a mighty crowd and great consumption of champagne.

I walked home with Speaker Blaine to his house and sat with him for an hour or so. To bed at 2.

Wednesday Dec 10.
WELCHER'S HOTEL, *Washington*—a bright fine day.

Mrs Ward Howe and Senator Bayard breakfasted with Sam and me, and we had a very pleasant time.

Afterwards I walked down to Alexander H. Stevens, whom I found by appointment a 10.30. I remained with him till near 12, though the heat of the room was excessive.

I then passed on to the House of Representatives and the Senate. Thence up to the room above where was Major Berley Poore who superintends the public printing. He has a very curious collection of autographs ranged with broadsides and prints under subjects such as Slavery. I looked this over while he was sending for some of the Congressional Reports for me. I left Washington by the 3.30 train, leaving Sam at the station and arrived at Baltimore about 5. Here I had a very pleasant dinner with Mr Otho Williams, his sister Miss Williams, his young daughter and son and two gentlemen whose names I forget. After dinner I left by the 11 oclock train for New York: where I arrived at 6.

Thursday Dec 11.

BREVOORT HOUSE, New York—fine but cold.

As soon as I had washed and dressed I went off to School no 35 in Thirteenth Street. I arrived about $\frac{1}{4}$ to 9 and was kindly received by the head master whose name I think is Forbes. At nine all the boys numbering a thousand of all ages and sizes defiled in to music on the piano. Then the master read a few verses of the Bible, said the Lord's Prayer, and the whole school sang a hymn from memory. Then the master announced the first declamation and a small boy advanced from the body of the school and stood next the master in front of me to declaim Aytoun's 'Death of Montrose'. When he began briskly

> "come hither, Evan Cameron,
>   and sit upon my knee"

one could not help picturing oneself the distrust with which Evan Cameron however small would have committed himself to so tiny a knee.

But the little chap declaimed very well, and I was sorry when he had done. Then a somewhat loutish lad came forward and declaimed some bombast from the early school of American oratory which if he take for the model of his own style he will infallibly move his contemporaries to much mirth.

I was much struck by the coolness with which these boys faced all their schoolfellows and spoke out. An English boy of their age would have blushed and giggled. Then the boys filed out to the sound of music, and the master and I afterwards walked round the classrooms. The method here used appeared to be almost discussion. In some of the younger classes a child would be asked "Now then what do you know of the State of New York?" and it would seem as if the shame of being found ignorant was sufficient stimulus. I say 'seemed' because I could not say positively of any and of course it would not be true of the great mass of boys.

The stimulus as punishment with the older lads seemed in many cases to be merely faint sarcasm: the astonished repeating of some of their answers. The position in life of the parents seemed fairly mixed: the son of Evarts and sons of other distinguished and well to do men were indicated to me. I could not believe that the boys were divided into classes so great was the difference of size and apparent age. But the master told me that the difference in stature and physical power between a Vermont boy and a New York boy was something marvellous; and that the homes of many of these boys were in Maine or Vermont.

After remaining in the school about an hour and a half I breakfasted, then called on Hurlbert. In the afternoon I walked with Mr Duncan who for a wonder was taking a holiday from his business. He shewed me all over the Knickerbocker Club which used to be his house.

In the evening I dined with the Duncans. It was the first dinner in their new dining room. Afterwards I went to a pretty little dance at Mrs Morton's given "to meet Miss Nellie Grant" or "the princess" as they call her here. There were a whole lot of old Etonians there and I am afraid we cronied together too much. Miss Morton niece of the house owner to whom Ernest Chaplin is engaged was in deep mourning for her mother and so did not appear; but Chaplin took me up to where she was sitting on the top of the staircase and introduced me. She seems charming. To bed at 2.30.

Friday Dec 12.
BREVOORT HOUSE, New York

At 7 this morning got up to go with Chief Justice Shea to West Point. It was very early, I was very sleepy. It had had no breakfast and the car was very hot; but I was talked to remorselessly in the two hours we spent travelling in the railroad from New York to Garrisons. We passed Washington Irving's cottage at Sunnyside, a quaint little building designed by himself, with walks laid out all round it.

At Garrisons we crossed the Hudson in a tiny ferryboat which took us to the foot of the steep hill on which Westpoint is built, and which seems the culminating point of that magnificent scenery which commences in the Palisades a row of heights forming one back of the Hudson.

Our party consisted of General Gillmore a very distinguished engineer officer, whose operations against Charleston were considered very remarkable, Shea Chief Justice of the Marine Court of New York, and a young Mr Colt no relation of the Revolver but very kind and pleasant.

We first called on General Rüger the principal of the college: "superintendent" is his title. He took us at once into the classroom on mechanics. As we entered eight or nine grey figures started rigidly upright. These were the cadets saluting the general. Comparative elasticity having been restored to their bodies we heard them, including a stout lowbrowed son of Brigham Young's, go through their demonstrations, which were Hebrew to me.

We then passed on to the Museum to see the model of the siege operations which General Gillmore conducted against Charleston:

meeting, as we did so several squads of students marching under the command of their officers from one classroom to another. For there is no individuality here and all is done in squads with automatic precision. After the Museum we went into the students rooms. Each room is occupied by two lads. All the furniture and decorations like their personal clothing is supplied by the institution so that no one may appear better lodged or better dressed than another. We only went into one room where a sick student was sitting. Everything had its place and was in its place with almost painful precision.

No student has any pocket money. Congress allows six hundred dollars a year to each pupil, which however is kept by the authorities. So that the uniformity here is almost the monotony of a prison. Each lad is dressed in the same grey suit with a good many globular gilt buttons on it. None is better dressed than another, for the same number of suits is supplied to each cadet by the authorities and may not be supplemented by private means. There is a barber who cuts their hair and blacks their boots, but he is not allowed to shave them: they must do that themselves. There are no holidays in the entire course of three years and a half, except a furlough of a month at the end of the second year. Nor can the students be said to have more than a bare hour a day for their own purposes.

I cannot imagine any place in the world where the principle of authority exists more completely than in Westpoint. It seems quite like an island in the United States.

We passed on to the riding school, and here we were met by General Upton commandant or second in command. Here the cadets were at exercise or rather about two dozen of them. The exercise was this. Two cadets go round the school in inverse directions. Each trots up to the first post and fires a pistol. He then starts off at full gallop, putting his pistol in its case and drawing his sword as he goes: at the opposite post he slashes at a cork on a post then going up the length of the riding school has at full gallop to sever a melon shaped object on the ground carry off with his point a ring suspended above him, shake that off and carry off with the point a cork from the next post. Two or three did the whole course completely but it requires great practice.

I think it was before the riding school by the bye that we went into the library where there is a very striking portrait of Jefferson one of the finest things I saw at Westpoint.

Then we went to the chapel which is so constructed as to make it appear that the worship is directed to the American eagle which is placed on some enormous stars and stripes aloft. Just as at Blenheim in the chapel there we are placed so as to appear to be adoring the great duke of Marlborough. In the Westpoint chapel the form of service varies according to the tenets of the chaplain who is I think appointed by the president. This is very characteristic.

Presently we went nominally to see Winfield Scott's grave really I think to see the magnificent view of the Hudson which is seen from the road to the churchyard. On our way there too was the fortress which Benedict Arnold had agreed to betray to the British. Scott's tomb was not worth seeing and the view was a fog.

At half past twelve General Rüger and General Upton gave us luncheon of which I was glad as I was beginning to be exceeding hungry. It was a delightful meal, the two generals were charming and genial and we were as hungry as wolves. It was broken up rather hastily, at my earnest request, that we might go and see the cadets at dinner. When we came into the hall the cadet captain gave the order to salute the two generals, and in an instant we were surrounded by several hundred grey pokers. I was taken up and presented to the three chiefs and found them delightful fellows, much delighted I think at having arrived within five months of the end of their course here. They consoled me a little for my ignorance by saying that mechanics was about the hardest nut they had to crack and that being past that year they had about forgotten all they had ever known. But this I fear was goodnature.

When the generals went out again, they all stood up once more: and we descended the hill to the ferryboat. At 4.30 we were in New York again.

My only regret in this delightful visit was that there had been a fog all day that shrouded the views, and that we had not been able to stay longer.

Colt walked home with me from the station. In the evening I dined with Chief Justice Shea again. All our party of the day was there—Gillmore and Colt, Gilchrist the Attorney General of New Jersey and his handsome wife, Judge Woodruff of the Supreme Court, Stuart, Mrs Shea two daughters and one son with his friend, a clergyman lineally descended from the first American bishop—I forget his name and one or two others.

Stuart and I drove home together.

Edward Balfour (who arrived here the day that I returned, with twenty five portmanteaux) Ernest Chaplin & I had oysters together afterwards. After which Balfour walked home with me and talked to me while I blinked at him from bed.

I ought to have mentioned that there are two negro cadets at Westpoint, but they are sent to Coventry by the others.

Saturday Dec 13.

BREVOORT HOUSE, New York—raining.

I hired a carriage this morning, as it was pouring with rain, and drove to Hurlbert's to Bouton's (the bookseller) to Kings to draw some money and to the Tombs to see the Warden.

In the afternoon I went to Tiffany's with Tarbat, and bought a flash[1] and a ring. After that I made some calls.

I dined with Belmont, Mrs Belmont, her daughter and her niece (I think), Miss Rodgers were the only ladies—they being in deep mourning. But there were lots of men—Duncan, Hurlbert, Barlow, Marble etc. I took in Miss Rodgers who is perfectly lovely and not yet out. She and I and Hurlbert, who sat on her other elbow, had 'a very good time'. After dinner we adjourned to the picture gallery till 11.45. Belmont has some lovely pictures

1. Tie pin.

notably a Gallait of the duke of Alva. Hurlbert and I had oysters afterwards.

Sunday Dec 14.

BREVOORT HOUSE, *New York*—very bright & cold.

I sat in writing all day till 3.30 when I went out, picked up Meysey Thompson at the Club, and together we went and left cards on the Stevens' and Kings.

I dined with the Barlows, and, like the last dinner it was a jovial and noisy meal. There was Mr and Mrs and Miss Barlow: there were the two Balfours, there was Marble editor of the 'World', there was Hurlbert principal contributor thereto, and there was Miss Travers a beauty by reputation. Much Madeira was drunk, much laughter was laughed, many jokes were joked. Afterwards several people dropped in. The two Balfours, Hurlbert and I eat the profligate bivalve at the club: and had pretty good fun.

It is odd how little all this seems on paper, when it was so pleasant in reality.

Monday Dec 15.

BREVOORT HOUSE, New York—fine.

Walked off with Ward to see Father Drumgoole at 53 Warren Street. To see that man in his little den is better than all Barrow's nine volumes of sermons. After that we went to the office of the Scottish American Journal, and then walked home. I then took Ward with Tarbat under Tiffany's invitation to me. Tiffany shewed us all over his store which is very beautiful. But what interested me most were the manufactures on the top floors—the jewellers and the engravers. It reminded one of the way in which one fancies that the great works of art were produced in the middle ages—by companies of artists working perhaps under the super-vision of Cellini himself. The silver plate with Japanese figures inlaid on it is the American work of which they are most proud here. But I did not care for it, any more than for the shapes of the other silver.

Afterwards I called for Miss Barlow, and we walked together to the house of a Mrs Cutting, a fascinating widow I was told, to whom she wished to introduce me. I was obliged to take the entire description on trust, as the room was so dark that I could see neither her fascinating face nor her widow's cap.

Thence we walked to Mrs Belmont's where I took leave of Mrs and Miss Belmont.

I dined with Boucicault where were Stuart, Hurlbert, Wikoff a great cosmopolitan theatrical character, and a gentleman whose name I never discovered. We had a very pleasant dinner, not too noisy, from which I was taken away to do a little of the nightside of New York with some detectives and the warden of the Tombs. This night side was disappointing and monotonous, so is not worth relating. Afterwards I went to the Patriarch's ball at Delmonico's. It was largely attended, and the cotillon or German was like a public meeting.

I did not get to bed till 3 oclock. Walked home with Mackerrell, or rather he with me.

Tuesday Dec 16.

BREVOORT HOUSE, New York—fine.

Father Drumgoole and Pat came before breakfast, and Hurl-bert and Stuart came to breakfast: when I presented Pat to Hurlbert.

After breakfast Stuart and I walked up to Sutherland's. Then I went to Duncan's for a moment, and called on General Porter who was out as usual. Then walked home buying a revolver at Reming-ton's on my way for Evy.[1]

1. Everard Primrose, Rosebery's brother.

After luncheon I called on Miss Gandy, and took her out. We first went to Tiffany's to ask after the ring, which had not yet come home, when lo! I fell in love with another with primroses on it and bought that too. We then went and called on the Barlows who were out and then took a good long stretch down Madison Avenue, to the Church beyond the Croton reservoir, when we turned into Fifth Avenue where the reservoir is, and walked back calling on the Stevens' who were also out. I then took Miss Gandy home. I shall not easily forget the way in which she told me about her father's ruin in the panic: which she at first thought was utter, but which afterwards turned out to be less.

I called on Miss Beckwith (*afterwards Lady Leigh) and the Duncans. I dined with Hurlbert at the Manhattan. Only Stuart and Dr Hamond were there, the treacherous Sam having thrown us over. However we had a pleasant dinner, and it seemed quite early when Duncan came to fetch me away to, the 'Mysterious' Ball, given at Dodsworth's. It was a very pretty small dance, with as usual the unending 'German'.

Hurlbert had asked me to supper and had told me to bring my friends. So I brought Johnny Balfour and Thompson: but there was no Hurlbert. So I entertained them and at last about 1.30 the traitor appeared. We did not go to bed till between 2 and 3.

Dec 17

BREVOORT HOUSE, New York—a lovely morning.

I was honestly grieved at the dawning of this day. I got up at 7 and packed up till 9 with the assistance of the waiter and Pat who came to say goodbye.

At 9 Tarbat and I went to breakfast with Stuart: there being another gentleman there whose name I did not catch. Then more packing and writing of letters and paying of bills and weeping over Sam's detention at Washington.

Then Hurlbert and I went to be photographed in the character of 2/3 Mendacious Club: an empty chair representing Sam. I was also photographed alone.

At about 1 we started and found ourselves at about 1.45 again on board the good ship 'Russia' in New Jersey. There was a crowd to bid me goodbye—Johnny Balfour (but where was Aleck?), Tarbat, Allan, Hurlbert, Stuart, Ward (Dufferin's aide,) McKerrell, Meysey Thompson and more—only my pen will not linger.

Disinterested beings! they had hardly been there a moment when it was hinted that it was customary for the Parting Guest to distribute champagne. So in an instant my cabin (the Chief Steward's) was transformed into a hideous scene of Bacchanalian revelry.

Mr and Mrs and Miss Duncan were there to say 'goodbye' to Aleck, and a very heartrending goodbye it was.

We were to have started at 2.30 but it was past three, when a tug had the impertinence to drag us out stern foremost. And presently we anchored—the fog was so thick. And anchored we remained all night within call of New York, with the blowing of mystic horns round about and the gleaming of phantom lamps and a general foggy feeling of depression.

Dec 18. Good ship 'Russia'—fog in the morning—a lovely afternoon.

Gradually this morning Staten Island became clear to us, quite close; and at 3.5 p.m. we began steaming up the glorious narrows. It was a lovely afternoon.

Dec 19 Friday—G. S. Russia—fine and calm.

At noon today we had made 260 miles from Sandy Hook.

Aleck and I sit next each other at table and I am immediately on the captain's left hand. On Aleck's left is Elliot—Melgund's brother —known as 'Snuffy' in my time at Eton. On the captain's right are two English girls—two Misses Potter with their father Mr Richard Potter the president of the Grand Trunk Railway.

Dec 20 Saturday. G Ship 'Russia'—fine.

A very fine day but a good deal of roll, so that remembering that it was only the second day of the voyage and besides that I had a good deal to do with this blessed journal, I remained in my cabin most of the day.

But why these elaborate explanations. No one will believe them. Posterity indeed will swear that I was ill. Well let them.

Sunday Dec 21. Good ship 'Russia'—fine.

To day we made 328 miles (i.e. our run at noon).

Mr Mitchell a newly ordained Universalist minister of Dunfermline read prayers, which I did not attend.

In other respects the day may be said to have committed suicide, to have finished itself without any special assistance on my part.

It is chiefly notable for my introduction to Golden Buck—a dish much celebrated on Cunard Steamers—consisting of two poached eggs perched on a Welsh rabbit or rarebit.

I mention this in case the dish should hereafter be mentioned and I from forgetfulness should eat of it again.

Monday Dec 22. The 'Russia'—cold and grey.

We now think we valued ourselves too highly yesterday. We took an observation today, which we were unable to do yesterday: and by that we make out that though we have gone like the wind since yesterday, and indeed faster, we have only made a score of 312. So we have to pay by today's humiliation for our triumph of yesterday.

It would be difficult to make any incident out of today. I get on pretty well with Stephens' 'Compendium of American History'.

Captain Cook our commander here has had a romantic story. His father was a wealthy banker in Waterloo Place, but was ruined in the great panic of 1825. His wife and eight children were left with the £10,000 which was settled on her, and went to the backwoods of Canada. Our skipper went as a middy of thirteen into the old East India Company's service. Having been in that eight years he entered this service till he had worked to the top of the tree. It is a rule of this Company that no one can command one of their ships, till he has commanded some other ship. So he went and served with another company for some years and then returned to this. He is an excellent captain. I should mention besides that he has had two very unfortunate marriages.

Dec 23. Good ship Russia—grey.

A brisk breeze, a grey morning with the Atlantic very cold rolling at atlanticky. I had a long talk with a little Scots trader from Dunfermline, who told me among other things that three fourths of the trade of Dunfermline in damasks and tablecloths was with the United States. He says that Dunfermline is a growing and thriving place.

I had also talks with Mr Potter and Judge Parsons and a ramshackle sort of philosopher Whitehouse the son of the Bishop of Illinois.

Dec 24. Good ship Russia—a lovely day.

If it were not for a certain superstitious feeling I should have written instead of "good ship' 'that wily beast the Russia'.

Verily, inscrutable are the ways of ships. We had a fair wind yesterday, the current was in our favour, the screw made more revolutions than she has made since we started—every thing was propitious (except that capricious flirt the ship) and our run is only 320 miles. Mr Ashmore one of the passengers took us down today to see the engines and the furnaceroom. The Chief Engineer a shrewd pleasant Scotsman from Glasgow told me that the American coal they get is much inferior to the English, that with the American they can only do 53 revolutions where with English coal they would do 55. 55 is the best they can do. He told me that mill hands are crossing by five hundreds at a time back from America to England. He also told me that the Clyde ship-builders cannot execute their orders to time now, owing to the supremacy of the artizan. He also told me, returning to coal, that they had never got such good coal from America since the war. They burn about 94 tons a day, but would burn less if the wind were unfavourable, and they lay in 1250 each voyage.

To day is a lovely day as lovely as a day well can be in these latitudes at this time of the year, a good deal lovelier than I have seen it in December in England. And it is Christmas Eve, and the boys and the virgins, as Horace would call them, shew a hankering for Christmas amusements. On a strict analysis of their wishes it appears that one boy desires mincepies and plenty of them, that one virgin (bluish) would like Shakspeare readings only who is to give them ?, that another boy is willing to be prompter if somebody else will act, and that the boys and virgins are unanimous in declaring their anxiety to form an audience on the interesting occasion. I have suggested (being called on) a return to James the First and Paradise and ideas of that sort, a light unconventional dance round the maypole, with the cunning thought, that, if the sea is rough, that will be the first and last of our Christmas festivities. I foresee a renewal of the controversy at dinner, for which I hear the bell now ringing, and think as my plan has been scouted that I had better side with the Blues. Firstly, because it is well to be on the side of the Virgins however azure. Secondly because a good deal of quiet fun may be got out of an æsthetic and controversial virgin who has not an idea of when she is talking nonsense: and thirdly —but Shakespeare and the Musical Glasses—I can't and there's an

VIII.   THE PRISON PEN IN THE TOMBS

IX.   THE NEW YORK TOMBS

end of it. Let them have their Yule log and their Boar's Head. By the bye an impartial Nero would be required to select that delicacy in our saloon.

Mr Potter does not think that Canada will ever become part of the United States. He says that he has noticed in the last five years a strong increase of dislike to the States in Canada. He says that the Canadians are offended by the annoying and corrupt administration of the American Custom House. Then of course he urges that the American debt is three times the Canadian. Then the Canadians see a great deal of the corrupt working of the legislatures in the states adjoining Canada. The French especially hate the U.S. This is all very well, but Canada is not homogenous: the French are as clearly separated from the other Canadians as any nation can be from another nation. The American debt will soon be paid at its present rate, and Canada will have neither the support due to a province from its government, nor the graces of independence nor yet the consciousness of power and propherity. She has no coal, she has an inclement climate, she does not realize as every state in the Union does her government. She has a parliament, but its decrees are liable to be put aside as the orders of a minor by a distant and unsympathetic guardian. Will she not come to feel this an intolerable position of servitude, will she not come to feel that her loyalty and devotion are treated by the mother country with at least inattention, will she not come to contrast the position of her inhabitants who have no share interest or consideration in the imperial government under which they live with the individual sovereignty of each citizen belonging to her neighbour. As to this point indeed I suppose that if it were possible to secure some more direct representation of Canada in Great Britain the Canadians would rather belong to England than to America. But that does not seem to be considered practicable, and in the absence of that, with a long exposed frontier and a strictly divided nationality, possessing besides interests and social institutions kindred to those of the Union, it does not seem to be at all probable that Canada will keep out of it.

I was interrupted here.

5

Dec 25. On board the 'Russia'—a lovely day

A bright laughing sky, a bright dancing sea, a cloud of gulls hovering about with some vague instinct of Christmas boxes, these are our Yule decorations. Beyond Nature's efforts we have no festivities.

Aleck indeed administered dough pills full of Cayenne pepper to the gulls, but that was only an incident. Our run is only 305, and is so far a disappointment if anything could disappoint us after yesterday.

We are only 67 passengers of whom I have realised very few. There is Mr Potter with two daughters, there is Aleck Duncan, there is Snuffy Elliot, there is Mr Ashmore; two young Gilmours a Whitehouse and sister, Judge Parsons, Mr Romsey and an anonymous American complete our table. I know no one else except a little Dunfermline Scotsman called Donald who has crossed some forty or fifty times. Then there is Mr Mitchell the Universalist minister, but he is in the second cabin and I neither know him or see him, so I suppose speaking scripturally that he is feeling very like the whale when he first swallowed Jonah. Then there is a Mr Smith, a partner of Mr Younger the brewer of Edinburgh, and whose father used to rent Moorfoot of my grandfather, who came and introduced himself to me after toddy-time tonight.

Dec 26. On board that sulky beauty 'the Russia'—a lovely day and a divine night.

Our run gets less and less only 288 today. O Russia, copper-bottomed, swift sailing, ironclad, why this dalliance with the waves. Thy sailors and lovers stand afar off and say "Her bottom is foul". Out upon the supposition! Dost thou leave America unwillingly or approach the dull shore reluctantly or art thou weary and sulky with the damnable iteration of thy voyages? or it, that must be it—that in England Christmas bills await thee?

Whatever it be I forgive the jilt. It could forgive my eldest brother, if I had one, today. A Sun, beaming soft as a Madonna of Raphael on the dimpled radiance of the Sea, moved with a fantastic freak of benevolence has only disappeared to make way for a more enchanting night.

Such a night! A moon high in the heavens, sending a steady line of radiance ever towards our ship, like the pillar of fire which guided the children of Israel, and she daintily, solemnly, as if conscious of divine protection and special tutelage paces through the hushed ocean, like Diana stealthily stalking a deer. All the world is moved to rhapsody and sentiment, and we feel that the moon is gracious alone to us, as if she were not equally illuminating the Kremlin and the Alhambra the ruins of Persepolis and some little smack coasting between Great Grimsby and Yarmouth, putting any astronomical question aside which I cannot pause to decide on.

All the world is moved, on board at least. There are very few on the deck. The doctor is hugging his romance, gazing at the sky and leaning on the mast, even the Universalist discourses his parasite in hushed voice. (All the world has a parasite, even I would set one up, only that after a month's duty he would go into a consumption or demand a rise of salary or do something unfeeling). The words "take it into your sairious conseederation" which escape Mr Mitchell are tolerably prosaic, but then so are not his long unshampooed hair, his unpatriarchal beard, his unromantic spectacles, his unepiscopal crozier, for such appears to be a stick with an ivory handle carved I think with a bas relief of a cockfight, probably presented to him by an admirer in the backwoods.

Having no romance to cherish and no sycophant to discourse and nothing if I had one to say to him, I turn my attention from a very practical pair of lovers who are reclining against the captain's cabin door, and think, for some inscrutable reason, about Homer: and wonder if he knew himself and felt his own sublimity. As whether he was simply lifted up by the deeds of dead heroes into verse, and as he heard the shouts and saw the tears with which his ballads were greeted he only thanked the Gods that men were left to appreciate godlike actions and for that they enabled him to describe clearly those superhuman beings to frail mortals: not thanking them that he had written the greatest of all poems, or at most only grateful that the diving sheen of those sublime heads had reflected some little inspiration on his verse, and that by continual gazing on the figures of the gods and their like he had become something superior to other men himself. At the same time I feel confident that he did not wear that fillet which he is made to wear in his portraits and which was never worn by any mortal being except my aunt's old maid and then only to keep on her false front.

To bed, vile scoffer! N. B. this is written the day after, when all excitement about Homer has worn off, and he seems to the vague eye merely a sort of primitive Catnach. After all the Newgate Calendar has heroes who would not be out of place in Homer, and Homer sings demigods who if they had once got into Newgate would have had the greatest difficulty in getting out. What though Homer's patrons battered each others' saucepan helmets, standing up in one horse shays while they exposed their neat and inoffensive tigers to a miserable death? Homicide, o shade of Homer is Homicide.

Dec 27. On board that — — — 'the Russia'—a day the immediate ancestor of a lovers' night.

My raptures and my vocabulary are alike exhausted. Everyday is the most beautiful day I ever saw. If I go on calling out "Swan, swan," dim suspicions will begin to arise than an old gray goose waddled in occasionally which I either did not see, or affected not to see. Today was the sort of brisk yet soft day on which one could vault a gate make a speech or propose to a woman with equal lightness of heart and disregard of consequences.

To night the sea glides gently away eel-like from our prow, just as a virgin who loves shrinks from her sweetheart for fear she should openly show her passion. And even the screw sounds more like a lute than a screw and the mute music of the stars and the waves is as vivid and as present as if it were a barrel organ to which you had contributed half a crown weakly and weekly to leave you alone. Vain effort! it was tried by the Lower Empire against the barbarians some years ago and has never, never been considered a success. We have seen the Wolf (I think) lighthouse and we soon shall see Fastnet and send up rockets. And then in time we shall see our homes and children and christmas bills, For us the torpescent tea and the merry muffin; we shall find out dear home unaltered, but, as the plumber casually suggests, sadly wanting repairs. We shall find our placent wife unaltered; only a little older and perhaps if possible more inclined to exercise authority, from having held power for the last three months unchecked by even that feeblest of second chambers, her husband. We shall find our offspring much as usual snivelling and affectionate, clamorous for Christmas presents, disagreeably affected by the absence of pocket handkerchiefs and the influence of catarrh, having grown beautifully, that is to say, having outgrown their old clothes and demanding immediate outfits from head to foot. And last but not least we shall rejoin our friends, all delighted to see us again, anxiously enquiring if we have suffered much for we are so sadly changed, and above all "to tell us all about America—have you learnt to speak through your nose and chew tobacco? And ain't you glad to be back in dear old England?" Dear Old England being wrapped in fog and your domestic blessings combined with unanimous welcomes wrapped in blue envelopes from the family tradesmen having deprived you of breath, you pause to reply; and are at once put down as a traveller without observation as an affected humbug, as a Yankeefied ass or as a cantankerous and ungrateful scoundrel.

Dear old England! Land of my birth and my prejudices, if I show no excessive rapture at seeing you again it is not from ingratitude. If one in my position for whom and for the likes of whom the whole blessed constitution of the country has been laboriously constructed and kept in repair, were ungrateful to England, it were vain to look for gratitude in this world. But as I get nearer to you the struggle between duty and pleasure becomes more apparent or rather pleasure shows its fenian head in spite of martial law, and the blockade announced by virtue is constantly broken by ease—

which—like all blockade runners—is English. Hora novissima, tempora pessima, nos laboremus. The hour is late, the times are evil, let us at any rate put our shoulders to the wheel.

Today I accosted the Universalist and had a long and interesting conversation with him. His is the second Universalist congregation in Scotland so far as I can make out. (*There is a church at Larbert, none yet at Dunfermline). But there are 23 in England and 973 in America, or 973 ministers. The story of his going to Dunfermline is curious. He was established at Larbert, but went over one day to preach at Tillicoultry, and returning, missed the evening boat from North to South Alloa. Whereupon he minded him that he had never seen the ancient abbey of Dunfermline. So he went off there instead of sleeping at Alloa. Observing several churches in the town, he went to a bookseller's and looked over a directory to see what sects had places of worship there. While thus employed, a voice from over his shoulder said to him "And pray to what religion do you belong?" Mitchell explained that he held a mixture of the tenets of the Calvanist and Armenian churches. To make a long story short, it turned out that forty five years before that a Universalist preacher, Mr Wall I think, had come to Dunfermline, made several converts and baptized one child. The man who accosted Mitchell, was that child, a wealthy man and owning the Music Hall the largest hall in Dunfermline. In this Mitchell preached, formed a congregation and has since remained there.

The Universalists believe in God being Love, and disbelieve in eternal punishment. They believe that the wicked suffer punishment both positive and negative in this world, and that probation is not over in the next. They do not mean "that Paul and Nero will jostle each other in the heavens"

We are great humourists on board. One gentleman a Pole has sat in full dress on deck throughout the whole passage in case of a collision, when he would be ready at once to jump into a boat.

To night there was to be an incident. So we sat up till two oclock in the morning to hear our screw stop for ten minutes and see the tender come alongside at Queenstown. Patient, suffering Screw, for thee my heart has always bled. While we sleep or while we wake thy toil is never ending. And when in a heavy sea a great wave comes and lifts thee from the water, I seem to hear thee gasp "at last—rest—at last". But on down to mid-ocean art thou plunged for thy eternal work compared to which the labours of Sisyphus were childish. I sometimes fear that like Samson thou, O Screw, mayest end thy bondage by a bloody revenge.

First incident—appearance of a rocket stick on deck where it struck perpendicular, as no other straight line ever did out of a proposition in Euclid.

Second incident, Queenstown at two oclock lay glimmering on shore, and an active little tender came to give to some letters and newspapers, to all a Pilot, and to take away three passengers. Never were parting guests so speeded as they were. Their luggage was bundled, and they were huddled almost kicked into the boats—and the wretched screw went at it again.

Judge Parsons, Mr Potter and I were engaged till then discussing a new club we want to get up in London for the special benefit of Americans. After the tender incident (this sounds like a flirtation) we broached a bottle of champagne and I read elegant extracts from the Times to them till 3.30 pausing to smile over the end of the Virginius—no right to fly American flag—paper obtained by perjury—and all the survivors to be immediately prosecuted: pausing to grieve over the appaling degradation of Desart, a person whom I do not know; but out of mere humanity I could not but feel sorry at the miserable depths he has contrived to plumb.

Sunday Dec 28. Partly spent on board the Russia—'dull'.

To night at about nine all our hopes were crowned and we landed. Elliot, Parsons and I supped gaily at the North Eastern Hotel. On the next morning we started by the 7.20 train to London. As I was waiting to get the tickets a richly dressed nobleman came up and said to me "If you want the third class it is round the other side". Blood will tell as the Tories say after dinner, so I must have looked republican.

And so my dream is over. I suppose I have been there but can I be sure. At any rate I am back in England. Miserably smoky and narrow as ever. Is it a dream that I have been in a country where all are born equal before the law? Where every man has the means of obtaining the dearest object of the Anglosaxon's heart, a plot of land of his own on which to live and die? Where each son of the soil carries in his wallet not the staff of a field marshal, for field marshals are abhorrent to the spirit of the country, but a possible passport to the White House, to the Bench of the Supreme Court, to every eminent position without exception that the State can afford. Where none as in heaven is before or after another, where none can afford to shut himself up in the shallow exclusiveness of wealth, lest he be left fixed though not a star, where every Citizen is a conductor of the electric spark of political power. It is easy to taunt and to deride, to point to a small vulgarism here and a petty venality there, and then to denounce the whole state as one stinking mass of corruption. The blotches exist indeed but they are the blemishes of the growing youth which are the virile promise of a coming beard and a splendid manhood.

But after all let us reduce the whole subject of contention into a single issue and abide by it. Lay before the world the exact advantages offered by every state to its inhabitants, and where would they go? We know already, for all uncared for humanity flows there now and does not return—to the United States. By that single test it seems to me that the merits of the United States as a community are sufficiently tested, and overwhelmingly established.

Appendix

CORRESPONDENCE of S. J. Ahern, The Revd. Fr. John Christopher Drumgoole, George Gore Ouseley Higgins, The Hon. Francis Charles Lawley, Henry Wadsworth Longfellow, Samuel Ward, and the 5th Earl of Rosebery, relating to his 1873 visit to North America.

★   ★   ★

I

LAWLEY TO ROSEBERY   *Trannick, Penzance.*
                                      August 18th, 1873.

Your letter has reached me here, and I hasten (having more time than in London) to send you a few American letters and hints. . . .

Now, as regards the United States I shall assume that you do not intend to start until after the St. Leger and that you will sail about the 16th or 20th of September. When you arrive in New York you will find any of the five inclosed letters (1 to W. Stuart, 2 to Hurlburt, 3 to Sam Ward, 4 to Willy Duncan, 5 to Belmont) sufficient for your purpose, but I think it possible that the 2 last (Duncan and Belmont) may not have got back to the United States by the 1st of October, as they are both in Europe at present. But my advice to you would be not to linger longer in New York on first landing but to go at once to Niagara—stay there 2 or 3 days and thence via Detroit to Chicago. From Chicago I would go to St. Louis—thence by rail to Cincinnati and then back by the Baltimore and Ohio

Railroad to Washington where you ought to be about the 1st of November. If you have a fortnight to spare in October it would be profitably spent in Canada; but I shall not send you letters to Sir John Macdonald, Sir Hugh Allan and other leading Canadians, until I know that you want them.

As regards Hotels in New York, it is customary for young English swells, to whom money is no object, to go to the Brevoort House. It is a good but old-fashioned and very costly Hotel, and I should counsel you to go par préférence to the Fifth Avenue Hotel which is a typical American caravanserai. On arriving there write your name down in full "the Earl of R.   London, England", and do the same wherever you go. Modesty and self abnegation are always misinterpreted by the Yankees. Ask for a bedroom with a bathroom attached. It costs, I think 1 dollar per diem more, but adds enormously to your comfort. It is a good plan, when you go to the eating room to take your first meal, to give the waiter who attends you a dollar or two, and to bid him look after you while there. Be courteously peremptory with waiters everywhere, but be prepared to shake hands with everybody except waiters. Especially with the conductors of railway trains, to whom you should always get introductions and give cigars, when you can.

I will send you some other letters, in addition to the five in New York herewith inclosed, in a day or two. Meanwhile a few words as to the 5 men named on the five accompanying envelopes.

1. William Stuart, an Irishman—real name Edmund O'Flaherty —once M.P. (for Dungarvan I think)—and a great friend of Ouseley Higgins. He left England in 1855 in money difficulties (not without some suspicion of forgery, between ourselves) in connection with Gregory, now Governor of Ceylon, poor Dunkellin and others. He is a wonderfully kind-hearted generous Irishman—not strictly veracious—but very fond of English swells—a devoted admirer of Gladstone—and once a warm friend of Thackeray. I believe it impossible between ourselves for him even to return to England though he sometimes talks vaguely of it. He is a great lion in the theatrical world of New York—always hard up, but always

bountiful—in fact a characteric and mysterious son of the Emerald Isle. He is much liked in New York.

2. Sam Ward: age nominally 53, really 68, celebrated old political wire-puller; has run through ½ a dozen fortunes: is cultivated and highly educated man—an excellent linguist—in fact an enigma. He makes much money wire pulling and lobbying—lives on the rail between New York and Washington; is a great friend of Billy Russell, Sala and many more English litterateurs. He will give you letters to every part of the United States when you may need them.

3. Hurlburt: The most distinguished and visionary journalist in the United States. Now connected with the New York World. A man of immense but erratic information: a charming talker; a little mad.

4. Willy Duncan: a Scotchman—a very money making successful Banker and very hospitable.

5. August Belmont: supposed to be natural son of one of the elder Rothschilds. A snobbish little Jew—with nice (but cold) wife and daughters. Very rich and purse-proud. Get a letter to him from Meyer or Anthony R[othschild]. Is one of the leading Turfites of the United States.

You may have as much hospitality as you like in New York with these letters. If you would like to make a detour between St. Louis and Cincinnati and to dip into Kentucky to see some of the great blood-stock farms there Belmont will give you a letter or letters to the chief men or Stuart will obtain them for you.

I will write again and send more letters in two or three days.

★   ★   ★

2

ROSEBERY TO HIGGINS   *Cataract House, Niagara Falls,*
                                                  October 21, 1873.

... I hope you are going well on this the day of the Cambridgeshire. I wonder if Dover furnished a favourite for the race. I am absolutely without news—not having seen an English paper (except one Pall Mall Budget of Sept. 27) or letter since I left England, more than a month ago. I have thus lost sight of England and have become completely American. Civis Americanus sum. However, though in the United States at this moment, I am in sight of the dominions of Victoria by the grace of God. I wrote to dear Huby from Salt Lake, as I fancied from his manner in England that he contemplated settling there with the Collector's wife and a few others of that kind. The climate there would not suit you. The first day the heat was so great I could not move: the second day there was six inches of snow.

I left New York this day fortnight and have only been four nights in bed during all that time; and one of those nights was spent in the bed of a Mormon Bishop who had several wives. Need I say that my moral feelings did not allow me to sleep? The curses of travelling here are the stove-heat of the carriages and the babies. Every carriage reeks with children of ages varying from two days to three years. The first receive natural nourishment in a disagreeably public way, the second will seek food in any part of the carriage under your legs or in your hat. Moreover they howl abominably, which is I suppose why they all grow into practised public speakers.

Would you like to hear my feelings on seeing Niagara? They are embodied in a hundred and forty five sonnets of which the copyright is reserved.

The people here are wonderfully kind and pleasant. My own private impression is that in their heart of hearts they like England very much. But the public prints always select England for those comparisons which we know are odious . . .

I left a card and a letter on Stewart or O'Flaherty but he has not responded. I hear he is much changed and very down on his luck. Sam Ward (to whom Frank Lawley gave me a letter) is charming: he is something like an old and short Sir Peel with the same inimitable twinkle of the eye: but of course he is on no level with his majesty . . .

★   ★   ★

3

WARD TO LAWLEY   *Brevoort House,*
                                          Fifth Avenue.
                                   December 23rd 1873.

I have been derelict in thanking you for the great unexpected happiness your introduction of our dear Rosebery shed upon my wayward and shadowy life.

He has won diamond opinions everywhere—in Salt Lake, Canada, New York, Boston, Washington he awakened affection and left regrets.

I enclose a paragraph from the New York Herald of Sunday the 21st Inst. four days after his departure. So thorough is his modesty that he would never show it to any one and I therefore give it to you to make such use of as shall seem proper.

Bayard and the rest of us often talk of you and all of us remember the sad beams of your pensive countenance . . .

★   ★   ★

4

LONGFELLOW TO WARD   *Decr. 31, 1873.*

I enclose the second chapter of the "Roman du Parapluie Perdu", which promises to become interesting.

As regards the "Tamer of Horses", I would not on any account enter into an agreement to furnish a series of papers; but I might perhaps lend him my Pagasus for a single heat, if he should make the offer you suggest.

Since your charming visit, I have been shut up with a cold, that has quite upset me for the time. I am gradually working it off, however, and hope soon to be myself again.

I see the Russia has arrived safely; and your young Lord has come to his own again.

A messenger rides up and down,
Through Beacon Street in Boston town;
From Craigie Hall unto the Club
Of Somerset; there at the Hub.
  Where is my Umbrella!

Then out and spake a blackamoor,
Porter at the great front door;
"Why do you so loudly ring?
And what means this bothering?"
  Where is my Umbrella!

And out and spake an Alfagin,
With his beard so white to see;
"Stranger, thou art justly served,
Stranger, this hast thou deserved."
  Where is my Umbrella!

Bearded men and children small
Weep their loss in Craigie Hall;
Ladies, with dishevelled hair,
Weep what tears they have to spare.
  Where is my Umbrella!

⋆   ⋆   ⋆

H. W. Longfellow, Esq.,   *Somerset Club,*
                                              Boston

Dear Sir,

I regret exceedingly that the umbrella you lent Mr Ward should have been lost or mislaid while in charge of the club.

May I trouble you to purchase a new one which will be entirely satisfactory to you, and when advised of the cost I will send you the money.

                    Yours Very Respectfully
                    R. M. Pratt
                    TREASURER.

5

LAWLEY TO HIGGINS   *Florence, Italy*
                                     2 Jan. 1874

. . . I inclose you a slip from a Washington newspaper of Dec. 7 which has just reached me and which I doubt not was sent by Sam Ward, to whom I gave the young man a letter of introduction and who is the most hospitable of entertainers that the United States boast. It is evident that "the Hearl" is enjoying himself, but Heaven grant that the affection with which he is regarded by the American girls may not be reciprocated by him, for most of them are the most heartless worldly b—s that can be imagined . . .

★   ★   ★

6

AHERN TO ROSEBERY   *The Oaks, Madison Avenue,*
                                     Elizabeth, N. J.
                                     24 Dec. 1873.

. . . I have published a little screed in our local paper which I take the liberty of sending your Lordship . . . I intend making your goodness the subject of an article in a Catholic journal in an adjoining City.

THE ELIZABETH DAILY JOURNAL—*Wednesday, December 24, 1873*

LOCAL MATTERS

A Liberal Earl and a Lucky "Pat".

A correspondent sends us the following which he vouches for as true:

The Earl of Rosebery, an English Peer, has been travelling recently in this country: he was heard of in Washington society, but he made his great mark in the city of New York.

There is a St. Vincent's Home for boys in Warren street and the Earl visited it, and was much interested in the good the Rev. Father Drumgoole is accomplishing there. The Earl became interested in a little ragged but prepossessing boot black which he saw at the Home, and he set the Father to work to make suitable enquiries as to the boy's worthiness. The boy was found to be the son of a poor widow, and one of seven children and a good boy who visited the Home often for religious instruction. The Earl upon this state of facts, charged the Father with the boy's education, and placed money at once in his hands for the purpose. Last week the Earl started for home, writing on the eve of his departure, a very kindly letter to Father Drumgoole, giving his address in London that the father may know where to call for money for Pat from time to time. In a P.S. the Earl requests the father to "devote a little of Pat's money to having him photographed," and direct a copy sent to him in London. Pat will be an Irish American lion in the British capitol.

Pat's occupation is gone, his brush and box are thrust aside; he will no more cry out to us who carry red-mud to the big city, that for ten cents he will "take the Jersey off, sir;" nor will he offer to "shine 'em up and black your moustache for ten cents!" The kind-hearted and heaven-sent Earl has changed all that for "Pat". doubtless a thorough education and a profession, with a nest-egg to start life on are the good things in store for the boy.

It is time the English returned the visits of the Americans in Europe who crowded their highways and by-ways, and spent money as free as water; let the visits be returned, but above all, if they have any more Roseberys over there, let us by all means have them. They do good to the individual and lucky "Pat"; they bring credit to the race; they make us all more kindly.

The readers one and all will join us in wishing a safe journey home to the Earl of Rosebery.

★   ★   ★

7

DRUMGOOLE to ROSEBERY

St Vincent's Home, 53 Warren St,
New York, Feb 2d, 1874.

Owing to the cloudy weather we have had almost all the time since you left, I had to wait over four weeks for "Pat's" photograph. I deeply regret this delay in complying with your kind request of writing to you and sending the picture.

The work is progressing rapidly.

The impetus which it has received from your visits and letter to me, is perceptible more and more every day. You have raised it from obscurity, and placed it in the most favorable light before the whole community, and promoted this cause, dearest to my heart, at least five years in advance of its natural growth.

The kindness and honour you have bestowed on me, a poor humble priest, has awakened in my heart a new and a holy love for you which I have never before felt for mortal man.

Your memory is always before my mind, and you are my constant companion at the holy altar every morning and I hail your presence there with joy even at the most solemn part of the Mass; for you come not to distract but to give me a new cause of thanksgiving to God for His goodness and mercy to us and directing your steps to my humble home; and when gazing on your countenance which was always illuminated with virtue and joy when visiting me, I pray to God, that He in honour of the precious blood of His Divine Son, which is mystically flowing at that awful moment, may pour down His choicest blessing upon you and enable you by your noble virtues and heroic deeds of charity to add new lustre to your noble name and race, and win a crown of eternal glory for your immortal soul.

I pray that this spiritual union between you and me will continue as long as God permits me to say Mass.

I was delighted with your photograph received through my good friend Mr. Hurlbert, and I regret that Mr. Sarony, the Artist, says I cannot get a large copy from it.

Pat entered the Jesuit College of St. Francis Xavier, 15th St. immediately after the holidays. At first he felt a little embarrassed but in a few days he began to be quite at home; he gives great satisfaction to his teachers and appears to get along nicely in his studies. He visits me every evening and I must say that he is a very good boy; I am very much attached to him and can say from personal observation that he is in every respect worthy of your kindness and appreciates it highly.

The following is a summary of his annual expenses:

Tuition	$64
Clothing	60
Books	12
	$136.

His expenses up to the present time including tuition paid in advance to April 19th 1874 have amounted to $56.40 leaving a balance on hand of $43.60 of the hundred dollars deposited with me.

I send you a few newspapers and enclose "Pat's" photograph and the prospectus of the College he is attending.

Your Lordships Grateful and Obedient Servant.

Part Three

Biographical Notes

THE following list is of the more prominent persons mentioned in the journal. The abbreviations in italic denote the sources of the information. See page 183 for the full list of sources.

Agassiz, Alexander (1835–1910)
Born at Neuchâtel, Switzerland and went to America in 1849. Zoologist, oceanographer and mine operator. *D.A.B.*

Allan, Sir Hugh (1810–82)
Born in Ayrshire, and went to Canada in 1826. Five years later he had joined the shipping firm of which he was to become the head. Allan was one of the original projectors of the Canadian Pacific Railway and in 1872 he was given a contract by the Macdonald government for its construction. When his large contributions to the campaign funds of Sir John Macdonald's party were made public, the fall of the government in 1873 brought the contract to nought. *D.C.B.*

André, John (1751–80)
The son of a Genevese merchant settled in London, André, a major in the British army, was adjutant-general to Sir Henry Clinton, commanding British forces in North America. Captured while arranging the surrender of West Point with its commander, Benedict Arnold, to the British, he was hanged as a spy. The

British army went into mourning for him, and a monument was put up to his memory in Westminster Abbey. *D.N.B.*

Arch, Joseph (1826–1919)

Younger son of a farm labourer of Barford, Warwickshire, he began work at the age of 9. Soon after his marriage in 1847, while continuing his work as itinerant skilled farm worker and hedger, he became a Primitive Methodist lay preacher. In 1872 efforts were made to start a trade union for agricultural workers, but the movement did not gather impetus until the next year, when Arch addressed a meeting. He was appointed organizing secretary of the National Union, and devoted himself to it until 1886. Arch was elected Liberal M.P. in 1882, and 1892–1902. The Union declined and disappeared, and with it Arch's influence. *D.N.B.*

Arnold, Benedict (1741–1801)

American revolutionary patriot and traitor. *See note for André, above.*

Arthur, Chester Alan (1830–86)

He performed important administrative duties during the Civil War, and his value as member of the Republican organization was recognized by President Grant who appointed him collector of customs of the port of New York in 1871, which post he held for 7 years. Vice-president in 1881 he succeeded to the presidency on Garfield's assassination the same year, but failed to be re-elected in 1884. *D.A.B.*

Astor, William Backhouse (1792–1875)

Son of John Jacob Astor I, on whose death in 1848 he succeeded to the rank of richest man in the United States. *D.A.B.*

Astor, William Waldorf (1848–1919)

Son of John Jacob Astor IV, he married in 1878 Mary Dahlgren Paul of Philadelphia. It was said that the contest between his wife and his aunt for leadership of the "four hundred" of metropolitan society contributed to Astor's dislike of his native land. In 1890, he moved to London, in 1899 became a British subject and was created Lord Astor of Hever in 1916. He bought *The Observer* in 1911, as well as other journals and newspapers. *D.A.B.*

Aylmer, General Lord (1775–1850)
Governor-general of Canada 1831–35, Lord Aylmer's family appear to have been established in Canada since that time.

Baby, Louis Francois Georges (1834–1906)
Represented Joliette, 1872–80, and member of the Macdonald cabinet during the last two years of that period. Afterwards a judge. *D.C.B.*

Barker, Benjamin Fordyce (1818–91)
New York professor of obstetrics, probably the best known physician in his field of the time, he developed a partial paralysis of the vocal cords and often was only able to speak in a hoarse whisper. *D.A.B.*

Barlow, Samuel Latham Mitchell (1826–89)
Lawyer, achieving spectacular success as a mediator in financial disputes, he was also an enthusiastic bibliophile and art connoisseur, specializing in the early history of America. *D.A.B.*

Barrow, Isaac (1630–77)
Master of Trinity College, Cambridge, he was one of the greatest of the great Anglican divines of the Caroline period. The best edition of his sermons was that published by the Cambridge University Press, 9 volumes in 1859. *D.N.B.*

Bates, Joshua (1788–1864)

Banker, partner of Baring brothers. He gave $100,000 towards Boston public library, and was acknowledged as its founder and largest benefactor. *D.A.B.*

Bayard, Thomas Francis (1828–98)

Democrat, senator from Delaware; secretary of state, 1885, in President Cleveland's first term, and ambassador in London, 1893–97, during his second—the first time that ambassadorial rank had been conferred by the United States. *D.A.B.*

Beckwith, Frances Hélène Forbes

Daughter of N. M. Beckwith of New York, married as his first wife the third Lord Leigh (1855–1938). She died in 1909. *Burke's Peerage.*

Beecher, Henry Ward (1813–87)

Brother of Harriet Beecher Stowe. Congregational minister of Plymouth Church, Brooklyn, from 1847 till his death. His public career has probably not been equalled in conspicuousness and influence by any other American clergyman, according to the *D.A.B.*

Belmont, August (1816–90)

Born the son of a wealthy landed proprietor of Rhenish Palatinate he decided to enter the house of Rothschild at Frankfurt-am-Main at the age of 14. The financial panic of 1837 enabled him to set up, holding the Rothschild agency, on his own account in Wall Street, and he was soon one of the leading bankers. In 1849 he married the daughter of Commodore Perry, who "opened" Japan to western nations. During the Civil War he was able through his European connections to set forth the northern point of view. Apart from his political and financial influence he was a collector of paintings and *objets d'art*, and for many years was president of the American Jockey Club. *D.A.B.*

Blaine, James Gillespie (1830–93)
Speaker in the House of Representatives 1869–75, later senator and secretary of state, 1881, 1889–92. *D.A.B.*

Blake, Edward (1833–1912)
Liberal, prime minister of Ontario 1871–72, member of Alexander Mackenzie's government in 1873, later succeeding him as leader of the party. In 1892 he was elected Irish Nationalist member of the British House of Commons for South Longford. *D.C.B.*

Bonaparte, Jerome Napoleon (1830–93)
Grandson of Jerome, King of Westphalia, the major part of his career was spent in the service of the second empire in France. *D.A.B.*

Bonner, Robert (1824–99)
Born in northern Ireland near Londonderry, he went to America in 1839. In 1851 he purchased the *Ledger*, a magazine which he promoted by extensive and original advertisements. Cornelius Vanderbilt, it was said, had about everything he wanted except Bonner's horse, Dexter. *D.A.B.*

Boucicault, Dion (1820–90)
Born in Dublin, of uncertain parentage and varied marital experience, actor and playwright, he wrote or adapted 132 plays, seeking and usually finding immediate success. At this time he was at the height of his career. *D.A.B.*

Boutwell, George Sewall (1818–1905)
His efforts on behalf of Radical Republicanism were rewarded by his appointment as President Grant's secretary of the treasury. Although not a supporter of civil service reform he laboured diligently to improve the organization of his department and to reduce the national debt. *D.A.B.*

Bristed, Charles Astor (1820–74)

Graduate of Yale and of Trinity College Cambridge. He published the book mentioned by Rosebery in 1852, and in the same year *The upper ten thousand, sketches of American society.* *D.A.B.*

Brooks, Phillips (1835–93)

At this time rector of Trinity Church, Boston, this "radiant spiritual athlete" of majestic build, author of the hymn "O little town of Bethlehem", was elected bishop in the Protestant Episcopal Church in 1891. *D.A.B.*

Burpee, Isaac (1825–85)

Liberal, member for St John 1872–85, an independent supporter of the Macdonald government until its fall, he became its vigorous opponent thereupon, and accepted the ministry of customs from Mackenzie, 1873–78. *D.C.B.*

Butler, Benjamin Franklin (1818–93)

Lawyer, Republican, member of Congress 1866–75, he took a prominent part in the Civil War. Appointed military governor of New Orleans in 1862, his conduct was high-handed in the extreme. *D.A.B.*

Cadwalader, John (1805–79)

Judge, 1858–79: counsel frequently found it difficult to present an argument before him owing to his habit of constantly intervening. *D.A.B.*

Cannon, George Quayle (1827–1901)

His parents were converted to Mormonism in Liverpool, where Cannon was born. In 1842 he emigrated to America, and in 1859 was chosen an apostle of the Mormon Church. Delegate to Congress 1872–82, after Brigham Young's death no man in Utah wielded so great an influence as Cannon. *D.A.B.*

Carpenter, Matthew Hale (1824–81)
Republican senator from Wisconsin in June 1873 he unwisely discussed in a speech the two most dangerous issues of the day, the "salary grab" (in which he had joined), and the Crédit Mobilier. He was re-elected to the Senate in 1879. *D.A.B.*

Cartier, Sir George Etienne (1814–73)
Former prime minister; minister of militia and defence in the Macdonald government. Author of "O Canada! mon pays, mes amours." *D.C.B.*

Cary, Annie Louise (1843–1921)
American, she made her début at Copenhagen in 1868. From her first appearance in America as a member of Nilsson's concert company in New York she was one of the most celebrated opera and concert contraltos. She retired on her marriage at the age of 40. *D.A.B.*

Cary, Thomas Graves
Father of Alexander Agassiz' stepmother.

Cauchon, Joseph Edouard (1816–85)
A former supporter of Sir John Macdonald he resigned his seat in the Senate in 1872 and was elected to the House of Commons as independent member for Quebec. Member of the Mackenzie government, 1875–77. *D.C.B.*

Chambrun, Charles Adolphe
Legal counsellor at the French embassy in Washington, and author of works on law in the United States and France. [See article on his son in *D.B.F.*]

Chauveau, Pierre Joseph Olivier (1820–90)
Prime minister of Quebec 1867–73, speaker of the Canadian Senate 1873–74, and later dean of the law faculty, Laval University, Montreal. *D.C.B.*

Christie, David (1818–80)
Born in Edinburgh; Senator in 1867, and in 1873 secretary of state in the Mackenzie administration. Speaker of the Senate, 1874–78. *D.C.B.*

Churchill, Lord Alfred (1824–93)
2nd son of 6th Duke of Marlborough.

Cleveland, Chauncey Fitch (1799–1887)
Lawyer, governor of Connecticut 1842 and 1843. A strongly anti-slavery Democrat he bolted his party in the mid-fifties and joined the new Republican party, but returned to the Democratic fold after the war: Republican presidential elector 1860, Democratic presidential elector 1876. *D.A.B.*

Coffin, Thomas (1817–90)
Liberal member for Shelburne, 1867–78, and from 1873 a member of the Mackenzie administration. *D.C.B.*

Collins, William Wilkie (1824–89)
Novelist, in 1873 and 1874 he followed Dickens' example and gave public readings in the United States. *D.N.B.*

Conkling, Roscoe (1829–88)
Congressman from New York 1859–66, and senator 1867–81, from 1868 he was Republican leader in New York. *D.A.B.*

Constable, Archibald (1774–1827)
Edinburgh publisher of Sir Walter Scott, and of the *Edinburgh Review*. *D.N.B.*

Cox, Samuel Sullivan (1824–89)
Democrat, congressman from Ohio 1857–65, and from New York 1869–85. As a journalist, a glowing description of a sunset won him the sobriquet which Rosebery mentions. *D.A.B.*

Cunard, Miss

Possibly daughter of Sir Samuel Cunard (1787–1865), of Halifax, Nova Scotia, son of Abraham Cunard of Philadelphia. In 1838 he went to England and the next year founded the steamship company which secured a government contract for carrying mail between Liverpool and Halifax, Boston and Quebec. In July 1840 Cunard was given a public banquet in Philadelphia to celebrate the establishment of steam postal communication between America and Great Britain. *D.N.B.*

Cushing, Caleb (1800–79)

He played an important part in the settlement of the *Alabama* claims, the Treaty of Washington and the Geneva arbitration. Minister to Spain 1873–77 he averted the danger of a Spanish-American war over the *Virginius* affair. *D.A.B.*

Custis, John Parke

Stepson of Washington, his daughter married General Robert E. Lee. *D.A.B.*

Daly, Charles Patrick (1816–99)

Born in New York of Irish parents he received a scanty education, but was appointed judge at the age of 28. He remained a member of the Court of Common Pleas of New York City for 42 years, and was chief justice for the last 27 of them. *D.A.B.*

Delmonico, Lorenzo (1813–81)

Born in the Ticino, Switzerland, he emigrated to New York at the age of 19. Without capital or, at first, influential friends, within twenty years he made New York known the world over as a centre of good living. *D.A.B.*

Drumgoole, John Christopher (1816–86)

Born in county Longford, Ireland, he joined his widowed mother in New York and became a cobbler. Ordained a Roman Catholic priest in 1869, he took charge of a lodging house for waifs and strays in 1871. By the time of his death he was caring for 1600–2000 children. "From my experience", he said, "I find that with proper care boys can all be reclaimed." *D.A.B.*

Dufferin, Lord (1826–1901)
Succeeded his father as 6th Baron Dufferin, 1841; governor-general of Canada 1872–78; subsequently viceroy of India, and created Marquess of Dufferin and Ava.

Duncan, William Butler (1830–1912)
Educated at Edinburgh, New York banker 1851–75; president and chairman Mobile and Ohio Railroad Company. *W.W.W.A.*, Vol I.

Duncan, Jessie Wilton (1855–1934); later *Dame Jessie Phipps.*
Daughter of W. B. Duncan, married W. W. Phipps of Chalcot, Wiltshire, who died 1911. Alderman, vice-chairman, and chairman of education committee of London County Council between 1913 and 1926. *W.W.W.[B.]* Vol III.

Edgar, James David (1841–99)
Liberal member for Monck and chief Liberal whip during the crisis of 1873. Speaker of the Canadian House of Commons, 1896–99. *D.C.B.*

Evarts, William Maxwell (1818–1901)
Counsel in the Geneva arbitration, 1871–72, for settling claims against Great Britain by citizens of the United States for losses through the activity of Confederate cruisers built, equipped and manned in England. President Hayes appointed him secretary of state, 1877–81; senator from New York, 1885. *D.A.B.*

Ferry, Thomas White (1827–96)
Republican, senator from Michigan 1871–83. Ferry was the first, after the financial crisis of 1873, to suggest a remedy. On 2nd and 4th December he presented propositions to remove the mono-

poly features of the national banking system, to stop the contraction of too much paper currency, and to issue a low interest convertible bond. It is perhaps not surprising, though hardly admirable, that Rosebery was an unappreciative auditor of these proposals. *D.A.B.*

Field, Stephen Johnson (1816–99)
Justice of the United States Supreme Court 1863–95, on his retirement he had completed 40 years judicial service. *D.A.B.*

Fish, Hamilton (1808–93) D.A.B.
Lawyer, governor of New York State, senator, secretary of state for the whole of President Grant's two terms. *D.A.B.*

Franklin, Benjamin (1706–90)
When agent in London for the Massachusetts House of Representatives, he was denounced at a Privy Council hearing as a thief by the solicitor-general Wedderburn (later Lord Loughborough and Earl of Rosslyn), for purloining certain compromising letters of the governor of Massachusetts. The story that, for the signature of the 1783 peace with England, or of the treaty with France in 1778, Franklin wore the Manchester velvet suit last worn when Wedderburn denounced him, is stated by the *D.A.B.* to be without adequate supporting evidence.

Fraser, James (1818–85)
Appointed by the British government commissioner on education in North America in 1865, he was 2nd Bishop of Manchester, 1870–85. During his episcopate 99 new churches were consecrated. *D.N.B.*

Frelinghuysen, Frederick Theodore (1817–85)
Republican senator from New Jersey, 1866–69, and in 1871, he obtained a position of commanding influence in his party. Secretary of state 1881–85. *D.A.B.*

Frye, William Pierce (1831–1911)
Lawyer, member of Maine State Legislature and of the national House of Representatives 1871–81, and senator from then till his death. A strict Republican, and a thorough-going expansionist. *D.A.B.*

Gallait, Louis (1810–87)
Belgian history and genre painter. A painting of the Duke of Alva is in the Wallace Collection, according to Bénézit.

Gammell, Robert Ives (1852–1915)
Financier, son of William Gammell and Elizabeth Amory Ives. Member of Goddard Bros., and Brown and Ives, cotton manufacturers. *W.W.W.A.*

Garfield, James Abram (1831–81)
Soldier, congressman and president of the United States, the last chief executive born in the typical American environment of a log cabin. Representative from Ohio from 1863, elected senator in 1880 but, Republican leader in the House since 1876, he was inaugurated president instead, the next year. He was assassinated by a crazy lawyer, disappointed office-seeker. *D.A.B.*

Gilchrist, Robert (1825–88)
Attorney-general of New Jersey, 1869–75.

Gilman, Arthur Delevan (1821–82)
Important as one of the first American architectural eclectics. He built the first office building in New York with elevators. *D.A.B.*

Glass, David (1829–1906)
Represented Middlesex in the Canadian House of Commons, 1872–74; Conservative. *D.C.B.*

DINING SALOON OF THE HOTEL EXPRESS TRAIN Across the continent, on the Pacific Railroad

XI. A CHARACTER SCENE

Gould, Jay (1836–92)
Unscrupulous railroad speculator, and financier. *D.A.B.*

Grant, James Alexander (1831–1920)
Born in Inverness; physician to the governors-general of Canada 1867–1905; member for Russell, 1867, and for Ottawa, 1892–96. *D.C.B.*

Grant, Ulysses Simpson (1822–85)
General-in-chief in the Civil War, Congress revived the rank of general, unused since 1799, for him in 1866. Allowing himself to be nominated by the Republicans he was elected president in 1868, and for a second term in 1872.

Grattan, Henry (1746–1820)
Statesman and orator, member of the Irish and, after the Union, of the United Kingdom Parliament. *D.N.B.*

Hale, Robert Safford (1822–81)
Essex county judge 1856–64, congressman from Vermont 1865–73. *D.A.B.*

Harper, Fletcher (1806–77)
The ablest of four brothers, he founded *Harper's Weekly*, 1857, and *Harper's Bazaar*, 1867. In these journals "there might be questions of taste, but there must be none of morals" : Harper's weekly, 16th June, 1877. *D.A.B.*

Havemeyer, William Frederick (1804–74)
Sugar refiner, capitalist, mayor of New York 1845, 1848, and again in 1872. His last term was disappointing to his supporters. *D.A.B.*

Hincks, Sir Francis (1807–85)
Born at Cork and emigrated to Canada in 1831. Finance minister in Sir John Macdonald's government, 1869–73. *D.N.B.*

6

Hollin, Luther Hamilton (1817–80)

An advanced Liberal, member for Châteauguay, he declined to join the Mackenzie government of 1873, though he gave his loyal support. *D.C.B.*

Holmes, Oliver Wendell (1809–94)

In 1847 Parkman professor of anatomy and physiology, Harvard; from 1871 to his retirement in 1882, of anatomy only. Published the *Autocrat of the breakfast table* in 1857. His son, bearing the same name, was justice of the United States Supreme Court. *D.A.B.*

Hood, Thomas (1799–1845)

Poet, best known for *The song of the shirt*, published in *Punch*, 1843.

Howe, Julia Ward (1819–1910)

During the Civil War her home was a centre of anti-slavery activity, and it was in her tent, while visiting a camp near Washington, that she composed, to the tune of *John Brown's body*, "The battle hymn of the Republic." From 1870 the major part of her life was given to women's causes. *D.A.B.*

Huntington, Lucius Seth (1827–86)

Liberal member for Shefford, 1861–82, a vigorous opponent of confederation. In 1873 he preferred against the Macdonald government the charges in connection with granting the Canadian Pacific Railway charter, which led to the fall of the government. *D.C.B.*

Hurlbert, William Henry (1827–95)

Originally called Hurlbut, graduate of Harvard and of Harvard Divinity School, he entered the Unitarian ministry for a short time, writing hymns which were long in use. In 1866 he joined the New York *World*, having been a journalist since 1855. Editor-in-chief of the *World*, 1876–83. *D.A.B.*

Hurlbut, Stephen Augustus (1815–82)

Half-brother of W. H. Hurlbert. Lawyer, Illinois Republican congressman and leader; general during the Civil War. Charges of corruption and drunkenness were apparently not without foundation. Later minister to Colombia and to Peru. *D.A.B.*

Jennings, Louis John (1836–93)

From the London offices of *The Times* he became their correspondent in New York, and editor of the *New York Times*, 1867–76. He exposed the "Tweed ring" into whose hands the municipal government of New York City had fallen. After this he returned to England; elected M.P. for Stockport, 1885–86 and in 1892. *D.A.B.*

Joly, Henri Gustave (1829–1908)

Member for Lotbinière, 1761–85. Later assumed his mother's surname of Lotbinière. Prime minister of Quebec, etc. *D.C.B.*

Kasson, John Adam (1822–1910)

Lincoln's assistant postmaster-general, at whose suggestion the president called the postal conference at Paris in 1863, from which the International Postal Union sprang. Member from Iowa 1862, 1873–77, 1881–84. Minister to Austria-Hungary and to Germany. *D.A.B.*

Kirkpatrick, George Airey (1841–99)

Lawyer, elected to succeed his father in the representation of Frontenac in the Canadian House of Commons, 1870, until appointed Lieutenant-governor of Ontario, 1892–97. *D.C.B.*

Laflamme, Toussaint Antoine Rodolphe (1827–93)

Lawyer, and Liberal, member for Jacques Cartier constituency 1872–78, and of the Mackenzie government 1876–78. *D.C.B.*

Lawrence, William (1819–99)

Jurist and Congressman from Ohio, 1865–77. An earnest

advocate of all measures designed to secure civil and political equality. *D.A.B.*

Lawton, Alexander Robert (*1818–96*)

Savannah lawyer, elected senator from Georgia in 1860, he was a leading advocate of secession. As colonel of a volunteer regiment he seized Fort Pulaski, thus committing the first overt act of war. Quarter-master-general of the Confederacy in 1863. President Cleveland appointed Lawton Minister to Austria, 1887–89. *D.A.B.*

Lee, Robert Edward (*1807–70*)

The leading Confederate commander in the Civil War, he ended his days as President of Washington College, Lexington, Virginia. Lee was descended from the Coton branch of the Shropshire Lees. *D.A.B.*

Longfellow, Henry Wadsworth (*1807–82*)

According to the *D.A.B.*, he made Hiawatha too much like a Christian gentleman.

Lorton, see *Lawton.*

McDonald, James (*1828–1912*)

Member for Pictou, Nova Scotia. *D.C.B.*

Macdonald, Sir John Alexander (*1815–91*)

Conservative, largely instrumental in the constitutional reforms which resulted in the federal Dominion of Canada, and its first Prime Minister, 1867–73. By the latter date the Conservatives had lost their popularity, and were easily defeated on the question of the alleged fraudulent opportunities given to Sir Hugh Allan, for the employment of American capital in the building of the Canadian Pacific Railway. Prime Minister, again, from 1878 till his death in 1891. A memorial to him was unveiled the next year by Lord Rosebery, secretary of state for foreign affairs. *D.N.B.*

Macdonald, John Sandfield (1812–74)
  Canadian Liberal prime minister, 1862–74. *D.C.B.*

Mackenzie, Alexander (1822–92)
  Born in Perthshire, he went to Canada in 1842. Liberal member for Lambton in the Dominion House of Commons, the Canadian Pacific scandal gave Mackenzie his opportunity. On 27th October he moved an amendment to the speech from the throne to the effect that the conduct of Sir John Macdonald's ministry towards the Canadian Pacific railway charter had deprived it of the confidence of the country. The debate continued seven days, whereupon Macdonald resigned and Mackenzie formed a new government. He was Prime Minister for 5 years. *D.C.B.*

Macpherson, David Louis (1818–96)
  Conservative, Canadian senator from 1867, and speaker of the Senate 1880–82. In 1871 he was a rival of Sir Hugh Allan for the Canadian Pacific charter, and his failure to obtain it somewhat chilled his party ardour. *D.C.B.*

McVickar, William Neilson (1843–1910)
  At this time rector of Holy Trinity, Harlem, later bishop of Rhode Island. *D.A.B.*

Marble, Manton Malone (1835–1917)
  From 1860 night editor of the New York *World*; 1862–76, editor and owner. *D.A.B.*

Massey, Gerald (1828–1907)
  Son of a canal boatman, born near Tring, Buckinghamshire. He started work at the age of 8 at a silk mill. By 1848 he had published his first volume of poetry, and he later found employment as a journalist. Patronized by the mother of the second Lord Brownlow, Lady Marian Alford, at Ashridge, from 1871 he had developed an overwhelming interest in spiritualism. He went on three lecture tours in North America, the first September 1873 to

May 1874. The note by Lord Rosebery, written long after the text of the *Journal*, to the effect that Massey's real name was Mercy, is not supported by the *D.N.B.*

Mathew, Theobald (1790–1856)
Irish Franciscan priest, "the apostle of temperance", visited North America 1849–51. *D.N.B.*

Maynard, Horace (1814–82)
Professor of Mathematics, East Tennessee College, congressman from Tennessee, he was popularly supposed, on account of his appearance, to have Indian blood. *D.A.B.*

Melgund, Lord (1845–1914)
Succeeded as fourth Earl of Minto in 1891; viceroy of India, 1905–10.

Mitchell, Peter (1821–99)
He was a strong advocate of federation, and became on the proclamation of the Dominion of Canada in 1867 its first minister of marine and fisheries. *D.C.B.*

Mitford, Algernon Bertram (1837–1916)
Created Lord Redesdale in 1902. He was an authority on the Far East.

Montcalm, Marquis de (1712–59)
Captain-general and commander-in-chief of the French forces in Canada, 1756–59, he was defeated by Wolfe on 13th September 1759, and died of wounds the next day, before the surrender of Quebec. *D.C.B.*

Morrill, Justin Smith (1810–98)
Representative and senator from Vermont from 1854, for twelve and thirty-two unbroken years, respectively. Although the Morrill Tariff Act passed in 1861 was made, through amendments,

more strongly protective than he had desired, his tariff views were somewhat coloured by a traditional distrust of Great Britain. *D.A.B.*

Morrill, Lot Myrick (1812–83)
Governor of Maine; senator 1871–76; secretary of the treasury, 1876–77. *D.A.B.*

Morris, Gouverneur (1752–1816)
Representative from Westchester County in the provisional congress, New York, May 1775; minister to France, 1792–94. *D.A.B.*

Morrissey, John (1831–78)
Gambler, prize-fighter, congressman and state senator in New York. When he died he owned three-quarters of the gambling casino at Saratoga, one third of the racetrack and buildings, together with other real estate. *D.A.B.*

Musurus Bey [later Pasha], Constantine (1807–91)
Turkish ambassador to London, 1851–85. *N.L.I.*

Niblo, William (1789–1878)
Born in Ireland and emigrated to America in youth. Starting as a New York coffee house proprietor he went into the concert business in 1823, and opened Niblo's Garden at Broadway and Prince Street six years later. He retired in 1861. *D.A.B.*

Nilsson, Christine (1843–1921)
Swedish operatic singer; made her début in Paris in 1864, and became a leading prima donna in Europe and America. *Ch.B.D.*

O'Conor, Charles (1804–84)
Nominated for President of the United States by the "straight-out" Democrats, 1872. His popularity among southern Democrats was due to his belief in slavery as a "just, benign and beneficent

institution", and to his conviction that there was no constitutional justification for coercing seceding states. *D.A.B.*

O'*Flaherty, Edmund* (*1821–86*)

A commissioner of income tax in Ireland, 1852–54, he forged bills of exchange, and on detection fled to Paris. From 1854 he lived in New York as William Stuart; journalist and theatrical manager. *M.E.B.*

Oliphant, Laurence (*1829–1888*)

Author of *Piccadilly*; diplomatist, traveller and mystic, the details of his bizarre career, including his enslavement to the American Thomas Lake Harris, are too involved for the purposes of these notes. *D.N.B.*

Patteson, Thomas Charles (*1826–1907*)

Born in Wiltshire he came to Canada about 1858, and was called to the bar. In 1872 when the Toronto *Mail* was established as organ of the Conservative party he was appointed managing editor. In 1879, postmaster of Toronto. *D.C.B.*

Pease, Edward (*1767–1858*)

Started work at the age of 15 at his father's woollen manufacturing business, Darlington; one of the first railway promoters. By the time of the death of his second son Joseph Pease (1799–1872) nearly 10,000 men were employed in the collieries, quarries and ironstone mines owned by the family, in addition to those working in the wool and cotton works. Rosebery would have been familiar with this family and its position, for his stepfather the Duke of Cleveland's property lay near Darlington. *D.N.B.*

Piatt, Donn (*1819–91*)

After a varied career he entered journalism in 1868, and from 1871 to 1880 was editor of the *Capitol*, Washington, where Piatt's complete frankness and outspoken honesty made him one of the most formidable and conspicuous editors of his time. *D.A.B.*

Pierce, Charles Sanders (1839–1914)

At the age of twelve had set up his own chemical laboratory. 1861–91, in United States Coast Survey; lectured at Harvard and John Hopkins Universities. Although according to the *D.A.B.* the most original and versatile of America's philosophers and her greatest logician, he died in poverty. His papers were bought from his wife by Harvard, and after years of futile attempts to organize them publication was started in 1931. *D.A.B.*

Plumb, Josiah (1816–88)

Born in Connecticut and manager of the State Bank of Albany, New York, he settled in Canada at the end of the Civil War; represented Niagara in 1874. Friend and confidant of Sir John Macdonald, and speaker of the Senate, 1887–88. *D.C.B.*

Poore, Benjamin Perley (1820–87)

Commissioned major in the Civil War under General Benjamin F. Butler; editor of the *Congressional Directory*, clerk of the Senate Committee on printing public records. In his generation Major Poore was one of the most popular persons in Washington. He wheeled a barrel of apples from Newburyport to Boston State House in fulfilment of a bet. *D.A.B.*

Porter, David Dixon (1813–91)

Entered the Mexican navy as a midshipman, then serving in the same rank in the United States navy. He married George Anne, daughter of Commodore Patterson. In 1870 he was promoted rear-admiral; and was chosen to command the fleet assembled at Key West in connection with the *Virginius* crisis with Spain. *D.A.B.*

Porter, Horace (1837–1921)

Artillery officer, A.D.C. to General Grant during the Civil War; stayed with him to become his military assistant at the White House. Though he managed to keep his record clear of the scandals

6*

which beset the administration he resigned his post in 1872, and became local representative and vice-president of the Pullman Company, as well as promoter of elevated railway lines. Ambassador to France, 1897–1905. *D.A.B.*

Potter, Henry Cadman (1835–1908)

At this time rector of Grace Church, New York, he made his conventional, fashionable parish a centre of Christian work of every sort. Later he succeeded his uncle as Protestant Episcopal bishop of New York, and began work on the Cathedral of St John the Divine in 1892.

Potter, Richard (1817–92)

His grandfather and uncle were among the original founders of the *Manchester Guardian*. A country gentleman until the financial crisis of 1847–48 took away most of his income, Potter then invested in English timber yards, and other North American and European concerns. Chairman of the British Great Western Railway, 1863–65, and president of the Canadian Grand Trunk Railway, 1869–79.

The two Misses Potter accompanying him were his 2nd and 8th daughters, Catherine, later Lady Courtney of Penwith, and Beatrice, who was to marry Sidney Webb. Mrs Webb was recorded as thinking that her father's insistence on their company was due to his desire to avoid associations with some of the more objectionable members of American financial society. Stephen Hobhouse: *Margaret Hobhouse and her family*; Rochester, Stanhope Press, 1934, pages 41 and 46.

Prescott, William (1726–90)

Descended from one of the seventeenth-century settlers in Massachusetts; played a leading part on the revolutionary side, Bunker Hill, 1775. *D.A.B.*

Prescott, William Hickling (1796–1859)
Historian: *The conquest of Mexico,* and other works of equal stature. From 1814 he was only able to see with difficulty. *D.A.B.*

Primrose, Everard Henry (1848–85)
The last born of the family, Rosebery's younger brother; their mother devoted to Everard Primrose the affection with which she was not always so generous. He was one of the first children to be born under chloroform, and his mother was told "Your child will be born an idiot" by an over-anxious old lady.

Ravensworth, Lord (1797–1878)
Succeeded his father as second Baron; created 1st Earl of Ravensworth, 1874.

Remington, Eliphalet (1793–1861)
His father, a farmer, established a workshop powered by a water wheel, and from this basis the son built up the great business named after him. *D.A.B.*

Richardson, William Adams (1821–96)
Jurist, Republican secretary of the treasury, 1873–74. He failed to resist inflation in the panic of 1873 and the next year the House Ways and Means Committee demanded Richardson's removal on account of his part in the "Sanborn contracts". The president appointed him to the Court of Claims, to which he was well suited. *D.A.B.*

Riel, Louis (1844–85)
Leader of rebellions in north-west Canada in 1870 and 1885. In 1870 he escaped from the country on the arrival of Wolseley's force. In 1873 and 1874 elected to represent Provencher in the Canadian House of Commons. In 1874 on taking the oath he was expelled from the House, and declared an outlaw the next year. After the failure of the 1885 rebellion he was tried and hanged for high treason. *D.C.B.*

Robeson, George Maxwell (1829–97)

Attorney-general of New Jersey, 1867; Secretary of the Navy, 1869–77. Robeson Channel, Greenland, was named after him by the explorer whose finances had been provided by Robeson's department. *D.A.B.*

Rothschild, Lionel Nathan de (1808–79)

A baron of the Austrian Empire, which dignity had been conferred on his father. Financier and member of parliament. His youngest brother, who built Mentmore, Buckinghamshire, was Baron Mayer Amschel de Rothschild (1818–74), father of Hannah de Rothschild, whom Rosebery married in 1878. *Burke's Peerage.*

Ruger, Thomas Howard (1833–1907)

Son of an Episcopal minister; graduate of West Point, but resigned his commission in the Corps of Engineers and practiced law. During the Civil War he attained the rank of major-general of volunteers. Superintendent of the United States Military Academy, 1871–76. *D.A.B.*

Sade, Marquis [or rather Count] de (1740–1814)

He published *Justine* in 1791, but it was almost certainly written earlier in the Bastille where he was kept by his family until the French revolution under *lettre de cachet* after he had been condemned for *debauche outrée*. *M.B.U.*

Schurz, Carl (1829–1906)

Born near Cologne. As a student at Bonn he took a leading part in the German revolitionary movement of 1849, and was the daring rescuer of Professor Gottfried Kinkel from the fortress of Spandau. He was obliged to leave Germany, and in 1852 he went to America from London. Lincoln appointed him minister to Spain in 1861, but he resigned in order to undertake military duties during the Civil War, when he was promoted major-general. Senator from Missouri, 1869–75. Subsequently journalist; secretary of the interior, 1877. *D.A.B.*

Scott, Winfield (1788–1866)

By training a lawyer he became a regular soldier and was general-in-chief of the army by 1841. In 1846 to took command of the army in person, and entered Mexico City with his forces. *D.A.B.*

Sharp, John (1820–91)

Born in Clackmannanshire, he joined the Mormon Church in 1847 and left for America the next year. In 1856 he was ordained by Brigham Young bishop of twentieth ward of Salt Lake City, and was also a colonel in the Mormon militia. He undertook the railroad building part of Mormon enterprise, and in 1873 was president of the Utah Central Railroad. *D.A.B.*

Shaw, Miss Amy

Wife of Dr J. C. Warren, *q.v.*

Sheridan, Philip Henry (1831–88)

Graduate of West Point, with a brilliant career as Union commander during the Civil War. He received the thanks of Congress for his exploits in the Shenandoah valley. In 1873, commanding a division at Chicago, he was tentatively selected by President Grant to command the forces for invasion of Cuba, in connection with the *Virginius* affair. *D.A.B.*

Sherman, John (1823–1900)

Younger brother of General Sherman. Lawyer, Republican, elected by Ohio to Washington for nearly half a century. Formerly representative from Ohio, he was at this time senator; later secretary of the treasury, and of state. *D.A.B.*

Sherman, William Tecumseh (1820–91)

West Point graduate, regular soldier, banker, head of a military college, president of a St Louis street railway before the Civil War, he has been called for his part in that conflict the first modern general, by Sir Basil Liddell Hart. Appointed general commanding the army in succession to Grant, 1869–83. *D.A.B.*

Smith, Joseph (1805–44)

Founded the Church of Latter Day Saints, 1830, and published the Book of Mormon later that year. Adherents gathered at Nauvoo, Illinois, which attained an almost independent status with Smith as mayor. Polygamy was declared a revelation in 1843. An attack on Smith resulted in his destruction of the printing press responsible. In the uprising against the Mormons which followed Smith and his brother were arrested and then taken from gaol and shot. *D.A.B.*

Sprague, William (1830–1915)

Governor of Rhode Island, and senator. His wealth derived from the textile manufactury started by his father was all but wiped out in the panic of 1873. *D.A.B.*

Spurgeon, Charles Haddon (1834–92)

Baptist. By the time he was 22 he was the most popular preacher in London; minister at Newington Causeway metropolitan tabernacle from 1861 when it was opened until his death. *D.N.B.*

Standish, Myles (c. 1584–1656)

He was hired as a soldier of fortune to accompany the pilgrim fathers to America in the *Mayflower*, 1620, and became a principal member of the community. *D.A.B.*

Stephens, Alexander Hamilton (1812–83)

In 1843, representative from Georgia in Congress, he was elected vice-president of the Confederate States in 1861. He was re-elected congressman, 1872–82, and in the last months of his life was governor of Georgia. Rheumatism reduced him to crutches and a wheel chair. In 1872 he published a school history *A compendium of the history of the United States*. *D.A.B.*

Stewart, Alexander Turney (1803–76)

He was born in County Antrim of Scottish Protestant parents. After emigrating to America such was his success that in 1862 he opened an eight-storey building covering the entire block between North and Tenth Streets, Broadway and Fourth Avenue, the largest retail store in the world. He owned numerous other enterprises by the time of his death, and the mansion which he built on Fifth Avenue shortly after the Civil War was long regarded as the finest in America. In 1869 President Grant appointed him secretary of the treasury, but he was barred from taking office by a law prohibiting the holding of the post by a man engaged in business. *D.A.B.*

Stewart, or *Stuart:* see *O'Flaherty, Edmund*

Sumner, Charles (1811–74)
    Trained as a lawyer. Elected Senator in 1851, from the start he spoke against slavery. As chairman of the Senate Foreign Relations Committee during the Civil War his service was of inestimable value in keeping the United States at peace with Great Britain and France, when war with either of them would have meant disruption of the Union. It was said that the two most influential men in public life at the end of the Civil War were Abraham Lincoln and Charles Sumner. *D.A.B.*

Tarbat, Viscount (1852–93)
    He was the second son of the third Duke of Sutherland. His mother was created Countess of Cromartie, and on her death he succeeded to this title, by special remainder. *Burke's Peerage*

Taylor, John (1808–87)
    Born in Westmoreland he followed his parents to Canada in 1832 and was baptized into the Mormon Church in 1836. He and Willard Richards were with Joseph Smith and his brother Hyrum when they were shot at Nauvoo. He succeeded Brigham Young as third president of the Mormon Church. *D.A.B.*

Thayer, Eli (1819–99)
    Originator of the Emigrant Aid Company, and fervent advocate

for company colonization of new lands. Republican and Democratic Congressman for Worcester District, 1857–61, and 1874–78, respectively. *D.A.B.*

Thornton, Sir Edward (1817–1906)
Envoy extra-ordinary and plenipotentiary to the United States, 1870–81, subsequently ambassador to Russia and Turkey. *D.N.B.*

Thurman, Allen Granberry (1813–95)
Representative, and from 1867 to 1881, senator from Ohio. During the Civil War he wanted to preserve the Union, and believed that an appeal to arms would destroy it for ever. He was recognized as Democrat leader of the Senate, known there as "Old Roman". *D.A.B.*

Tiffany, Charles Lewis (1812–1902)
Opened shop in 1837 opposite City Hall, New York. By 1848 he had begun to manufacture jewellery, and for half a century his firm was considered leader of that trade in America. His son, Louis Comfort Tiffany (1848–1933), artist and glass-maker, began experimenting with coloured glass in 1875. *D.A.B.*

Tilley, Samuel Leonard (1818–96)
From 1867, Canadian minister of Customs, from 1873 of finance. *D.C.B.*

Tocqueville, Count Alexis de (1805–59)
His *Democracy in America* was published in 1835.

Todd, Alpheus (1821–84)
Librarian of the Parliament of Canada, 1867–84, and a minister in the Catholic Apostolic Church. Born in London, and went to Canada with his family in 1833. *D.C.B.*

Tupper, Charles (1821–1915)
Born in Nova Scotia, he studied and took his M.D. in Edinburgh.

Prime Minister of Nova Scotia 1864–67; member for Cumberland in the Canadian House of Commons, 1867–84, cabinet minister in 1870, and Prime Minister in 1896. High Commissioner in London, 1883–96, with a year's break in 1887–88. *D.C.B.*

Upton, Emory (1839–81)
  During the Civil War his career was notable for varied service and participation in a large number of engagements. Commandant of cadets and instructor in artillery, infantry and cavalry tactics, West Point, 1870–75, and originator of the system of infantry tactics named after him. *D.C.B.*

Verres, Gaius (c. 120–43 B.C.)
  Roman magistrate famous for his misgovernment of Sicily, prosecuted by Cicero.

Ward, Samuel (1814–84)
  Son of a banker and brother of Julia Ward Howe, by 1849 he had lost his fortune, and joined in the gold-rush. During the closing years of the Civil War and the administrations of Johnson and Grant he lived in Washington as a lobbyist in the employ of financiers interested in national legislation. *D.A.B.*

Warren, John Collins (1842–1927)
  Boston surgeon and founder of the Collis P. Huntington Memorial Hospital for Cancer Research there. *D.A.B.*

Watts, Frederick (1801–89)
  Farmer and lawyer of Carlisle, Pennsylvania; appointed federal commissioner of agriculture, 1871–77. *D.A.B.*

Webb, Alexander Stewart (1835–1911)
  Graduate, and later professor at West Point, major-general during the Civil War. 1869–1902, president of the College of the City of New York. He was much admired for his personal qualities, but made little original contribution as an educator. *D.A.B.*

Webster, Daniel (1782–1852)
Lawyer and statesman. In his speech of 7th March 1850 he said that slavery was not so great an evil as disunion. *D.A.B.*

Webster, Sidney (1828–1910)
Lawyer practising in New York. *W.W.W.A.*

Wedderburn, Alexander: see note for *Franklin, Benjamin*

Wickoff, Henry (c. 1813–84)
The date of his birth as well as his parentage was carefully concealed. Author, adventurer, British agent in Paris, 1850–51. Hero/villain of an attempted abduction of an American heiress, for which he spent 15 months in prison in Genoa through British influence, 1851–52. *D.A.B.*

Williams, George Henry (1820–1910)
Republican senator from Oregon 1865, attorney-general 1871–75. A Senate judiciary committee found that he had removed from office a district attorney, to prevent him from prosecuting for election frauds. It was said that his wife's new landau, also, furnished at public expense, helped to block her husband's promotion: for when President Grant nominated him chief justice in 1873 the appointment aroused such criticism that Williams asked the President to withdraw his name. *D.A.B.*

Williams, Roger (1603–82/3)
Puritan divine, president of Rhode Island. *D.A.B.*

Winthrop, Robert Charles (1809–94)
Descended from the first governor of Massachusetts, John Winthrop (1587/8–1649), congressman and senator before the Civil War, he retired into private life on its outbreak. President of Massachusetts Historical Society for 30 years. *D.A.B.*

Wolfe, James (1727–59)
Commanded the British expedition against Quebec in 1759; died during the battle on the Plains of Abraham, which resulted in the fall of the city *D.C.B.*

Wood, Fernando (1812–81)
Congressman, Mayor of New York. One of the Tammany Hall leaders, when ousted he formed his own personal following into Mozart Hall. He had a genius for political organisation, and in gaining and keeping power he was audacious, ruthless and resourceful. *D.A.B.*

Woodruff, Wilford (1807–98)
Became a Mormon in 1833; ordained apostle by Young in 1839, and in 1889 president. *D.A.B.*

Young, Brigham (1801–77)
Baptised into the Mormon Church in 1834, accepting the divine inspiration of Joseph Smith. On the murder of Smith in 1844 he at once proved himself the strongest personality among the Mormons, and was elected president of the Church in 1847. In 1850 Utah Territory was organised by Act of Congress, and Young was appointed first governor. Although President Buchanan sent an expeditionary force in 1857, Young refused to vacate office when displaced, and although he was forced to yield his successors were mere figureheads, Young governing effectively as before. *D.A.B.*

Yznaga, Consuelo (d. 1909)
Daughter of Don Antonio Yznaga del Valle, of Ravenswood, U.S.A., and Cuba. Married in 1876 Viscount Mandeville who on his father's death in 1890 became 8th Duke of Manchester. *Burke's Peerage.*

Sources for biographical notes

AMERICAN

D.A.B.   Allan Johnson: *Dictionary of American Biography*; New York, Charles Scribner's Sons; London, Oxford University Press, from 1928.

W.W.W.A.   *Who Was Who in America*; Chicago, A. N. Marquis, from 1943.

CANADIAN

D.C.B.   W. Stewart Wallace: *Dictionary of Canadian Biography*; Toronto, Macmillan Co, 2nd edition, 1945. Later editions are *Macmillan Dictionary of Canadian Biography*.

FRENCH

D.B.F.   J. Balteau, etc.: *Dictionaire de Biographie Française*; Paris, Librairie Letouzey et Ané, from 1933.

Bénézit.   E. Bénézit: *Dictionnaire . . . des Peintres, Sculpteurs . . .*; Paris, Libravrie Gründ, new edition, 1961.

M.B.U.   Michaud: *Biographie Universelle*; Paris, Desplaces, new edition, 1854.

N.L.I.   Claud Augé: *Nouveau Larousse Illustré*; Paris, n.d.

BRITISH

D.N.B.   Leslie Stephen: *Dictionary of National Biography*; London, Smith Elder, from 1885; Oxford University Press, from 1937.

M.E.B.   Frederic Boase: *Modern English Biography*; London, Frank Cass, 2nd impression, 1965.

Ch.B.D.   *Chamber's Biographical Dictionary*; Edinburgh, W. & R. Chambers, new edition, 1961.

W.W.W.[B.]   *Who Was Who*; London, Adam and Charles Black, from 1920.

Index

A FASHIONABLE P